FOODIES ACROSS THE POND

Two great friends sharing our love of all things foodie. We offer so much knowledge and experience, and have come together to share a pinch of it with you. We combine American and British traditions, ingredients, and of course, having fun with food.

We could fill a library of recipe books, but with our first cookery book, "*Twelve Menus of Christmas*," we offer you a book that you can dip in and out of. We hope you will find firm favourites inside it. We have created a collection of recipes that will impress, make life easier, avoid waste and give you some chill out time to enjoy the company of family and friends.

We encourage you to play with the recipes, we certainly do.

We hope that you enjoy reading, cooking and of course eating the food that you create from Twelve Menus of Christmas and that we become a fixture in your kitchen.

Have a wonderful, magical, and delicious Christmas!

love

Lisa and Jane

ABOUT JANE......

Welcome to my home in Herefordshire. A glorious county, tucked away just inside the border of England's gateway to Wales. The lush countryside provides us with a fabulous selection of the most delicious food and drink, and my waistline is proof of this. I live here with my son George, who regularly makes appearances in "Foodies" Video's and is invaluable when it comes to the editing. It is here that I run my business, Myrtle's Kitchen.

A massive perk of working in the foodie world, is meeting other artisan producers. I have made so many great friends through both making and sharing food.

Food is truly a gift and being able to share it with friends, the greater gift.

Work is mad for me during December, creating goodies to fill hampers, stockings and lots of food markets and fairs, thank goodness Christmas itself is quieter. Time to chill and unwind. When I was 14 years old, I offered to cook Christmas Lunch for my Mum as her gift and that was it, I'd created another tradition. Her favourite dish on the table was the parmesan parsnips. Me? I love all the trimmings, but my favourite bit is the leftovers with a great Christmas movie on Boxing Day!

love, Jane

ABOUT LISA.....

Welcome to my home in Washington! I'm originally from Southern California and moved to the PNW 16 years ago with my family. I've been married for 26....almost 27 years, have two kids in college (*one will graduate this December!*), and a sweet and energetic rescue pup.

I love my morning coffee (*and my afternoon lattes*), anything chocolate, traveling, creating content for A Menu for You, and I dream of retiring in the South of France.......or Hawaii.

The holiday season is a busy one, but I always try to focus on enjoying the small moments because they make the best memories. The cooking and baking (*and my kids helping while they're home from college!*), nibbling on cookies and eggnog in the afternoon, leftover pie for breakfast, watching ALL the Christmas movies on repeat, friends casually stopping by for drinks and cheese plates, and, of course, eating ALL the turkey sandwiches.....with extra cranberry sauce!

love, Lisa

MENUS

TWELFTH NIGHT : OR, KING AND QUEEN.
by Robert Herrick
Written 1660

NOW, now the mirth comes
With the cake full of plums,
Where bean's the king of the sport here ;
Beside we must know,
The pea also
Must revel. as queen, in the court here.

Begin then to choose,
This night as ye use,
Who shall for the present delight here,
Be a king by the lot,
And who shall not
Be Twelfth-day queen for the night here.

Which known, let us make
Joy-sops with the cake ;
And let not a man then be seen here,
Who unurg'd will not drink
To the base from the brink
A health to the king and queen here.

Next crown a bowl full
With gentle lamb's wool :
Add sugar, nutmeg, and ginger,
With store of ale too ;
And thus ye must do
To make the wassail a swinger.

Give then to the king
And queen wassailing :
And though with ale ye be whet here,
Yet part from hence
As free from offence
As when ye innocent met here.

A tradition was to bake a cake with a dried pea and bean in the
middle. Whoever discovers the bean will be King for the night and
the who finds the pea, will be Queen. Presiding over the party and
festivity, complete with crowns!

(Lamb's wool is Spiced Ale)

Lamb's Wooll - Wassail Punch

Twelfth Night

Historically twelfth night was a big deal, celebrated in England, Scotland and Wales, In Medieval times it was a 12 day event, culminating in a celebration on 6th January. Now we traditionally take down all of our Christmas decorations on this day.

The "Feast of the Epiphany" would take place, with feasting, dancing and singing. Acrobats, fools and jesters would entertain, and all of this would be watched over by "The Lord of the Misrule". (Love the idea of this role for a day!)

Monarchs would be dressed in their finery and gifts distributed and on the 12th night "Wassail" would be drunk, the drink of "good wishes", and the grand Wassail Cup would be passed around the merry makers.

INGREDIENTS:

- *6 cooking apples*
- *2 pints ale*
- *½ teaspoon ground ginger*
- *½ teaspoon grated nutmeg*
- *Runny honey to sweeten*

DIRECTIONS:

Preheat oven to 150'c

Place the apples into a dish with a little water and bake until moist and soft.

Heat the ale gently in a saucepan, then our over the apples. Add the spices and set aside for half an hour for the flavours to combine.

Strain through the sieve and return to the saucepan, reheat gently and then add honey to sweeten. This may be 2 – 4 tablespoons, depending on the ale and your tastebuds.

Try not to drink too much while checking.

Pour into your Wassail Cup and share.

Pudding Chômeur

This dessert is originally from Québec and the first time I ever had it was on vacation in Canada. It's a cross between a sticky toffee pudding and fluffy pancakes. It's incredibly rich, so a little bit goes a long way! Serve with ice cream or fresh berries to break up the sweetness.

INGREDIENTS:

- **Serves 8-10**
- **10 tablespoons unsalted European butter, room temperature (I love using Kerrygold)**
- **1 cup granulated sugar**
- **2 large eggs**
- **2/3 cup whole milk**
- **2 cups all purpose flour**
- **1 teaspoon baking powder**
- **2 cups maple syrup**
- **2 cups heavy whipping cream**

DIRECTIONS:

In the bowl of a stand mixer, beat the butter and sugar until smooth, about 2-3 minutes. You can also use a hand mixer, but I highly recommend pulling out the stand mixer for this.

Add the eggs, one at a time, fully incorporating each egg before adding the next one. Then add the milk and mix to incorporate.

Add the flour and baking powder, mix gently and slowly just until the flour is combined.

If you want to make this ahead, cover the dough and store in your fridge for 24 hours. If you're baking it right away there's no need to refrigerate the dough.

When you're ready to bake it, make the maple sauce. Add the maple syrup and cream to a medium saucepan, and bring to a boil. As soon as the mixture boils, turn off the heat and set syrup mixture aside.

Preheat oven to 425 'f / 220'c /Gas mark 8

Divide the dough, evenly, among six 8-ounce ramekins. Or put all the dough in a buttered 9x13 inch baking dish.

Pour the syrup cream mixture evenly over the six ramekins, or the baking dish. Place the ramekins or baking dish on a rimmed baking sheet. THIS IS REALLY IMPORTANT! The baking sheet will catch any spills.

Bake until bubbling, and lightly browned, about 20-25 minutes for the ramekins. If baking in a baking dish, you'll probably need to add an additional 10-15 minutes.

BAKING TIP: If your oven runs hot, start off the cooking time at about 10-15 minutes because it's easy to add extra time if you need it.

Butter lettuce with toasted Hazelnuts and Champagne Vinaigrette

INGREDIENTS:

- **1 head of butter lettuce, cleaned**
- **1/4 cup toasted hazelnuts, roughly chopped**
- **1 teaspoon Dijon mustard**
- **1 teaspoon minced fresh garlic**
- **1 teaspoon fresh lemon juice**
- **3 tablespoons champagne vinegar**
- **Kosher salt and freshly ground black pepper**
- **1/2 cup good olive oil**

DIRECTIONS:

In a small bowl, whisk together the mustard, garlic, lemon juice, vinegar, 1 teaspoon salt, and 1/2 teaspoon pepper. While whisking, slowly add the olive oil until the vinaigrette is emulsified.

TIP: Put all ingredients - dijon, garlic, champagne vinegar, salt, pepper and olive oil in a mason jar or container. Put the lid on VERY tightly and shake vigorously until combined.

Place the salad greens in a medium bowl, toss with about 1/2 the dressing. Sprinkle with hazelnuts, then toss again. Taste to see if you need to add more dressing.

Serve immediately.

DIRECTIONS CONT'D:

Preheat oven to 450'f /230'c /Gas Mark 8s. Make sure you have a really clean oven. If you don't, open a window (or two) and turn on your fan. Put the meat on a rack in a roasting pan. Roast the tenderloin for about 25 minutes until the internal temperature is 130 degrees F for medium-rare. When you insert your meat thermometer, put it into the thickest part of the meat. Remove meat from oven, place it on a cutting board and tent with foil. The meat will continue cooking while it's resting. Be sure to rest it for at least 10 minutes, to ensure the delicious flavorful juices stay inside the meat, and don't bleed all over your cutting board.

While the meat is resting, you can make the sauce.

In a small saucepan, bring vinegar, finely chopped shallots, tarragon, salt and pepper to a boil, until it has reduced, about 5-8 minutes.

Remove from heat, add the 4 egg yolks and whisk rapidly and continuously. Return to very low heat, continue to whisk, and remove from heat every 1 minute – repeat this process for 10 minutes, constantly whisking until the sauce becomes frothy and starts thickening.

By now your sauce should have reached its goal and become lovely and thick. Remove from heat and whisk it 1-2 tablespoons of butter at a time, waiting until fully incorporated before adding another 1-2 tablespoons of butter until you've added all the butter.

If you find the sauce is cooling and the butter isn't melting, put the pan back on the stove over low heat.

The key to success is to constantly whisk the sauce, alternating on/off the heat.

TIP: to be sure the pan is the right temperature, you should always be able to touch the bottom of the pan with your hand and it should be warm to the touch, but not hot.

When the sauce is finished, arrange the beef medallions on a plate, or large platter, spoon the béarnaise sauce over them and garnish with fresh parsley. Serve with mushrooms on the side -- or spoon mushrooms over the beef medallions before adding the béarnaise sauce.

Beef Tenderloin with Bearnaise Sauce and Caramelized Mushrooms

INGREDIENTS:

- **1 beef tenderloin roast (about 2 pounds), fat trimmed off**
- **12 tablespoons butter, divided into twelve 1 tablespoons slices**
- **¼ cup white wine vinegar (or Champagne vinegar)**
- **2 shallots, finely chopped**
- **4 egg yolks**
- **1 tablespoons chopped fresh tarragon2 tablespoons olive oil**
- **12 ounces/350g assorted mushrooms (use button, cremini, shitake), cut into large pieces**
- **Kosher salt, freshly ground pepper**
- **4 tablespoons unsalted butter, cut into pieces**
- **2 garlic cloves, crushed**
- **2 tablespoons chopped fresh Italian leaf parsley**
- **Garnish: chopped fresh Italian flat leaf parsley**

DIRECTIONS:

Make the caramelized mushrooms first -- you can easily reheat them right before serving.

Heat oil in a large skillet over medium-high until just beginning to smoke.

Arrange mushrooms in skillet in a single layer and cook, undisturbed, until bottom side is golden brown, about 3 minutes. Make sure the mushrooms are in a single layer, so they get the lovely browned color. If they are too crowded, the mushrooms will steam and won't brown. Season with salt and pepper, toss mushrooms, and continue to cook. Keep tossing often and, if needed, reduce heat to avoid scorching the mushrooms. Cook until they are golden brown on all sides, about 5 minutes more.

Reduce heat to medium and add butter and garlic to skillet. Tip skillet toward you so butter pools at bottom edge. Continually spoon butter over mushrooms until butter smells nutty, about 4 minutes. What you want to do is tip the pan, spoon the butter, give a stir and repeat. Remove mushrooms from skillet with a slotted spoon.

Pecan Chili Camembert

This is an easy starter for a party and is great sharing food. If you are entertaining more than 4 simply multiply the recipe. They look fabulous placed along a dining table. Equally lovely on a sharing board in front of the telly!

INGREDIENTS:

- **1 round (250g/10oz) Camembert in wooden container**
- **50g / 2oz pecan halves**
- **1 x green chilli (remove seeds and chopped)**
- **75g /3oz apricot jam**
- **Crackers or baguette to serve**
- **Olive oil if toasting baguette**

DIRECTIONS:

Preheat the oven to eat oven to 200C/180C fan/gas 6
Blend together in a small bowl, the jam, pecan nuts & chopped chilli.

Open the Camembert and remove the inner packaging, put it back into the box/container. Spread the jam mix in the centre of the Camembert and replace the lid.
Place on a baking sheet and bake and cook for 15 – 20 minutes.

Serve with crackers or with thinly sliced baguette.
If your baguette is not at its freshest, slice and place around the Camembert before it goes into the oven. Drizzle with the oil and cook with the Camembert, until golden.

NEW YEAR'S EVE

Jam Roly Poly

I admit to including this as a bit of fun, but after the fun you can eat a delicious dessert. In the U.K we have a long history of puddings: Clootie Dumpling, Spotted Dick, Trifle …. Roly Poly is one of my favourites.

I recommend using a great quality jam in this pudding, if you have time pop to your local artisan / farmers market to pick some up.

INGREDIENTS:

- **150g / 5oz self raising flour (plus a little extra for dusting the work surface)**
- **50g (2oz) caster sugar**
- **75g (30z) vegetable suet**
- **Grated zest of half an unwaxed lemon**
- **75ml / 3 oz semi skimmed milk**
- **50g / 2oz of a good quality raspberry jam or an alternative "tart" jam. I use Chuckleberry Jam**
- **40g / 1 ½ oz toasted flaked almonds (optional)**

DIRECTIONS:

Heat oven to 190'c / 375'f / Gas mark 5

Mix together the flour, sugar, suet & lemon zest in a bowl and then gradually incorporate the milk, bring together using a knife until the mix forms a soft dough. If you have milk left, set to one side.

On a floured surface roll out your dough to a large rectangle shape (30 x 20cm). Spread the jam to within 2cm of the edge of the rolled out dough. Sprinkle over half of the almonds.

Brush the edges with some of the spare milk and roll up the dough from the short end (a little like a Swiss Roll). Pinch the ends to help stop the jam escaping and then scatter with remaining almonds.

Butter a large piece of parchment, place on a baking sheet, carefully move your Roly onto the parchment seam side down and wrap tightly with the parchment. Twist up the ends.

Bake in the oven for 45 minutes.

Stand for 5 minutes and then transfer to your serving dish. Serve with home made custard (page)

One excellent thing about this dessert is that it can be made in advance & frozen. Once wrapped, add an extra layer of foil and freeze. It can be cooked from frozen for 1 hour 15mins.

Roasted Balsamic Vegetables with Mozzarella

This recipe is a real winner and just sits by the side of a dish or on it's own. You don't have to add the mozzarella. If you do, do not skimp on the quality. You will find that it will weld itself to your pan and prove a nightmare to wash up.

Select a colourful selection of vegetables. I suggest per person, but go for it, they can always be reheated later.

INGREDIENTS:

- *1x thin carrot cleaned*
- *¼ courgette cut into big chunks*
- *¼ red onion thinly sliced*
- *¼ aubergine slice into chunks*
- *¼ red pepper – deseeded and chopped into chunks.*
- *In addition to your vegetables, you will need*
- *1 tablespoon rapeseed oil*
- *1 tablespoon balsamic vinegar*
- *2 x clove of garlic, grated*
- *1 x buffalo mozzarella ball sliced*
- *Seasoning*
- *Fresh thyme*

DIRECTIONS:

Preheat your oven 200'c / 400'f Gas mark 6

Place all of your selected vegetables into one big ceramic (ovenproof) serving dish.

In a bowl, mix together the oil, vinegar and garlic.

Pour over the vegetables and give them a bit of a rub.

Sprinkle on sea salt and freshly ground black pepper and the fresh thyme. Cook in the oven for 30 mins.

Carefully remove from the oven and add the slices of mozzarella to the surface of the vegetables.

Return to the oven and cook for 10-15 mins until the cheese is soft and gooey.

DIRECTIONS CONT'D:

After 6 hours, remove ribs from slow cooker and put in a large bowl. Use a fork to pull the meat off the bones of the ribs, break the meat up into small pieces, and discard the bones.

Skim fat off the top of the sauce -- to make this even easier, put the sauce in the refrigerator overnight. The fat will rise to the top and be easy to scoop right off!

With an emulsion blender, puree the sauce (the liquid remaining in your slow cooker) until desired consistency. Reduce sauce by one third on medium heat, stirring frequently.

For the Polenta:

In a large saucepan, bring the water, milk and butter to a boil. Add 2 teaspoons of salt to the water and whisk in the polenta.

Whisk constantly for 3 to 4 minutes to prevent lumps. Simmer for 45 minutes, partially covered and stirring every 10 minutes, until the polenta is thick, smooth, and creamy.

Add the creme fraîche and Parmesan. Check for seasoning and adjust consistency by adding milk or water to the polenta. Polenta may be made up to 20 minutes ahead of time and kept covered until ready to serve.

Foodie Notes:

This recipe uses a slow cooker, but if you don't have one, you can make this in a Dutch oven and cook at in your oven. Preheat oven to 275 and cook 3-4 hours. If using in Instant Pot, pressure cook for 45 minutes, and natural release for 15 minutes.

Red Wine Braised Short Ribs with Creamy Polenta

INGREDIENTS:

- **3 pounds beef short ribs**
- **3 tablespoons olive oll**
- **1 medium onion, peeled & diced small**
- **2 carrots, peeled, trimmed & diced small**
- **3 cloves garlic, peeled & minced**
- **1 cup dry red wine**
- **1-2 cups beef stock**
- **1 (24 ounce) can chopped tomatoes**
- **1 tablespoon tomato paste**
- **1/4 cup chopped fresh parsley**
- **1/4 cup chopped fresh basil**
- **4 sprigs of fresh thyme**
- **1 teaspoon dried oregano**
- **Salt & Pepper**
- **POLENTA:**
- **4 cups water, plus more as needed**
- **4 cups milk, plus more as needed**
- **3 tablespoons butter**
- **2 teaspoons salt**
- **2 cups polenta, not**
- **1/2 cup creme fraiche**

DIRECTIONS:

MAKE THE DAY BEFORE FORE EXTRA FLAVOR!

NOTES: This recipe uses a slow cooker, but if you don't have one, you can make this in a Dutch oven and cook at in your oven. Preheat oven to 275 and cook 3-4 hours.

In a large heavy skillet or Dutch oven, heat the olive oil over medium heat and brown the ribs well on all sides. Remove ribs with tongs and place the ribs in your slow cooker. Don't wash out your skillet!!

Add onions and carrots to the skillet (the same skillet you used to brown the ribs) and cook for 3 to 4 minutes or until they take on color.

Add the garlic, and cook until fragrant.

Add the red wine and beef stock to the skillet, and stir well, scraping any browned bits off the bottom of the pan and cook for 3 to 4 minutes.

Pour the beef stock and wine and carrots over the ribs in your slow cooker.

Add the tomatoes, paste, parsley, basil, oregano, salt and pepper.

Turn your slow cooker on low for 6 hours. (If the sauce begins to thicken too much, add a cup of water or beef stock)

DIRECTIONS CONT'D:

Add a further 245g / 1oz butter to the pan and brown the shallots. Set to one side.

Add the flour to the pan. Stir continuously for 1-2 mins. Add the vinegar, jelly, port, stock and reserved marinade. Bring to the boil and simmer for 2 mins to thicken.

Return the venison and vegetables to the pan. Drain the jar of pickled walnuts and add. Season and add bay leaf. Cover with a tightly fitting lid. Once simmering transfer to a preheated oven: 180'c /350'f / gas mark 4 for 30 mins and then reduce the heat to 150'c / 300'f /gas 2.

Add the cranberries, orange juice & shallots and cook for 1 ¾ hours or until tender and unctuous!

Serving suggestion, a massive plate of roasted vegetables and pot of creamy mashed potatoes.

After cooking, this dish can be frozen and then reheated.

Venison Daube

This slow cooked venison dish is impressive to have on standby in the freezer. It is one that has been in my scrapbook for way too many years!

You do need to marinade the venison overnight, so it needs a little planning. But it's so worth it when you have this amazing dish to pull out of your freezer on a night you'd rather spend watching Christmas movies than in the kitchen cooking.

INGREDIENTS:

- *Serves 6*
- *1 kilo /2lb stewing venison cut into 4 cm cubes*
- *Marinade:*
- *100g /4oz chopped onion*
- *100g / 4oz chopped carrot*
- *100g /4oz chopped celery*
- *2 oranges*
- *4 garlic cloves, crushed*
- *1 x tablespoon dried thyme*
- *75ml / 3fl oz light rapeseed oil*
- *1 teaspoon black peppercorns, crushed*
- *Daube:*
- *500g / 1lb shallots*
- *2 tablespoon oil*
- *75g / 3oz unsalted butter*
- *3 level tablespoons of plain flour*
- *100ml / 4 fl oz red wine vinegar*
- *1 jar pickled walnuts*
- *2 level tablespoons redcurrant jelly*
- *250ml / ½ pint port*
- *250ml / ½ pint beef stock*
- *100g / 4oz dried cranberries*
- *Salt & freshly ground black pepper*
- *Bay leaf*

DIRECTIONS:

Prepare the venison to marinade overnight. Put the venison, onion, celery & carrot into a bowl.

Finely grate the orange rind and juice. Put the juice to one side. Add the zest to the meat along with the peppercorns, garlic, thyme & oil. Mix together, cover and refrigerate overnight.

The next day make the daube.

Heat the oil in a large flameproof casserole add 25g / 1oz butter.

Skin the shallots.

Drain the marinated meat mix, RESERVE the marinade for later.

Brown the venison in small batches in the casserole dish, then remove with a slotted spoon to a separate dish. Add more butter if necessary.

Once you have finished browning the venison, reduce the heat and sweat the vegetables for 2-3mins. Save with the venison.

Spiced Nuts

These are great to keep on hand to nibble on when you're cooking, or add to a cheese tray when the neighbors come over. Or, put them in tins and add to Christmas gift baskets.   If you want a little extra heat, double the cayenne pepper.

INGREDIENTS:

- *1/2 teaspoon ground cumin*
- *1/2 teaspoon cayenne pepper*
- *1/2 teaspoon ground cinnamon*
- *4 cups unsalted mixed nuts, such as walnuts, pecans, hazelnuts, and almonds*
- *4 tablespoons unsalted butter*
- *6 tablespoons brown sugar*
- *1 teaspoon salt*

DIRECTIONS:

Heat the nuts in a dry skillet and cook, stirring frequently, until they begin to toast, about 4 minutes. Add the butter and cook, stirring, until the nuts begin to darken, about 1 minute. Add the spices, the sugar, 1 tablespoon water, and the salt and cook, stirring, until the sauce thickens and the nuts are glazed, about 5 minutes.

Remove the nuts from the heat and transfer to a baking sheet lined with aluminum foil, separating them with a fork. Let the nuts stand until cooled and the sugar has hardened, about 10 minutes.

Store in an airtight container.

THE EXHAUSTED CHEF

Homemade Custard

Makes 1 pint of custard
If you have time indulge your family and friends and make this custard, you won't be sorry when you hear the "ooohs" and "aaaahhhs"

INGREDIENTS:

- **1 pint / 570 ml milk**
- **2 fl oz / 55ml single cream**
- **4 egg yolks**
- **1 oz /25g caster sugar**
- **2 level teaspoon cornflour**
- **1 vanilla pod or some good quality vanilla paste**

DIRECTIONS:

Put the milk, cream and vanilla pod into a saucepan and bring very slowly to simmering point over a low heat. Remove the vanilla pod.

Whisk the egg yolks with the sugar and cornflour in a separate bowl and blend.

Whisking all of the time with a hand blender or balloon whisk, pour the warm milk onto the egg mixture. Return the mix to the saucepan and once again, return to a low heat. If using vanilla essence or paste, this is the time to add it. Stir with a wooden spoon until thickened.

Pour into a jug to serve.

If you are keeping the custard warm, pop some cling film or parchment onto the surface to prevent a skin forming.

Mincemeat and Cranberry Tart

I recommend that you use a home made or artisan mincemeat from your local farmers market. It will have so much more flavour and be far less sugary.
If you are not a cranberry fan, you could substitute for cherries or raspberries.

INGREDIENTS:

- **500g / 1 lb Ready made puff pastry**
- **Flour for dusting surface**
- **250g / 10oz jar artisan/homemade mincemeat**
- **250g fresh cranberries**
- **1 Bramley apple**
- **Zest of 1 orange**
- **50g / 2oz light brown sugar**
- **1 tablespoon (15ml) orange liqueur**
- **1 egg**
- **Icing sugar for dusting**

DIRECTIONS:

Divide the pastry in half and roll out two rectangles, one slightly larger than the other. (About 30 x20 cm). Place some parchment on a baking tray and lay the smaller rectangle of pastry on it.

In a bowl mix together the cranberries, mincemeat, orange zest, sugar & orange liqueur.

Peel, core and grate the apple and add to the mixture.

Spread the mixture onto the pastry base leaving a border of about 2-3cm. Brush the border with beaten egg and then lay the larger piece of pastry on top, trim and seal the edges well.

Score a pattern into the top of the pastry using the tip of a sharp knife. Go to town with the Christmas theme!

Chill until firm.

Preheat fan oven to 200'c 400'f Gas mark 7. Glaze the tart with beaten egg and cook for 20-25mins. Dust with icing sugar and serve with homemade custard.

Bubble and Squeak

Hands up – feeling a bit of a fraud including B&S in my recipe selection, but surely it is a must have for Boxing Day? It certainly is in the U.K.

A great staple, its name derives from the bubbling and squeaking noises that it makes during the cooking.

It can be a real old mish mosh of left-over vegetables from your Christmas Day feast, but the staples are potato & cabbage (green not red, nobody wants pink Bubble & Squeak!) I am thinking Lisa's Truffle Potato Mash (page 80), would be an amazing addition.

A great side dish, so easy to cook which is equally delicious served for breakfast with crispy pancetta and poached egg. I need to move on as I am making myself hungry.

INGREDIENTS:

- *Vegetable Oil*
- *Knob of butter per serving*
- *Fresh parsley, washed and chopped*
- *Left over potatoes, mashed and roasted*
- *Left over green cabbage, shredded*
- *Left over chopped up vegetables*
- *Seasoning (sea salt & ground pepper – I quite like a white pepper)*

DIRECTIONS:

In a wide heavy based saucepan, heat up a generous drizzle of oil.

In a bowl mix together your vegetable/potato mix and some seasoning. Do not pulverise.
When your oil is hot, add your veg to the pan. Do not over fill, if there is too much mix, you will not achieve that lovely crispy potato. When your vegetables are browning, then turn the mix over in the pan and brown the other side.

It is as simple as that. Add to your serving plates and top with a nob of butter and sprinkle of fresh parsley.

Any remaining uncooked mix can be used for a pie topping with left-over meat.

Turkey Coronation Pie

I am an ardent chutney maker and a bit of a mango chutney snob, therefore I have to recommend using a great quality mango chutney in this pie, offering what's left in the jar on the side. When i started Myrtle's Kitchen, Mango Chutney was our first product and still has it's own fan club.

INGREDIENTS:

- *Serves 6*
- *500g / 1 lb block puff or shortcrust pastry*
- *About 500g / l lb of cooked leftover turkey*
- *1 onion, finely diced*
- *2 cloves garlic finely chopped*
- *2 tablespoons of your favourite curry powder (we used a mild madras)*
- *Pinch of cinnamon*
- *Pinch nutmeg*
- *Pinch ground coriander*
- *25g / 1 oz ground almonds*
- *100g / 4oz dried apricots, quartered*
- *3 heaped tablespoons of good quality mango chutney*
- *500m double cream*
- *2 tablespoon fresh coriander chopped*
- *1 tablespoon vegetable oil*
- *1 egg*

DIRECTIONS:

Heat the oil in a large pan. Fry the onion for about 5 minutes until softened. Add the garlic and all the dry spices and cook for a few minutes.

In a bowl combine the apricots, almonds, chutney, cream, mango chutney & turkey. Stir through the chopped coriander & season.

Pour into a pie dish.

Preheat the oven to 180 'c / Gas mark 6/350 f

Roll out the pastry and cut a circle that will cover the pie dish. Beat the egg and brush a layer around the edge of the pie dish. Lay the pastry disk over the filling mix in the casserole dish. Cut away any excess pastry and crimp the edges so that they look attractive.

Decorate with cut out pieces of pastry, cut a vent in the centre to enable steam to escape and glaze the whole surface with egg.

Cook in the oven for 30-40 minutes until golden brown and piping hot. Serve with fresh vegetables or a crunchy green salad.

Turkey Pho

INGREDIENTS:

- *Serves 6*
- *Time: About 1 hour*
- *2 medium yellow onions, halved and peeled*
- *1 (4-inch) piece of fresh ginger (do not peel)*
- *12 cups turkey or chicken stock, preferably homemade*
- *¼ cup fish sauce, plus more to taste*
- *1 star anise*
- *2 tablespoons brown sugar*
- *1 (1-pound) package dried rice vermicelli*
- *4 cups shredded cooked turkey (about 1 pound)*
- *Kosher salt, to taste*
- *1 large bunch of cilantro, chopped*
- *1 cup thinly sliced scallions/spring onions, about 1 bunch*
- *GARNISHES:*
- *12 ounces/340 grams mung bean sprouts (about 3 cups)*
- *1 small bunch Thai basil sprigs*
- *3 jalapeños, stemmed and thinly sliced*
- *2 to 3 limes, quartered*
- *2-3 carrots, grated*
- *6-8 of your favorite mushrooms, sliced (button, cremini, shiitake)*

DIRECTIONS:

Using tongs, hold onions and ginger directly over open flame of a gas burner for about 5 minutes, turning them occasionally, until they are charred on all sides.

To make it easier, char each ingredient one at a time.

If you don't have a gas stove, turn your oven to "broil" and set onions and ginger on a foil-lined baking sheet. Drizzle with a little olive oil. Broil, turning 3-4 times during cooking, for 15 to 20 minutes until charred on all sides.

Allow charred ginger to cool, then slice it into 1/2-inch coins.

In a large Dutch oven, combine onions, sliced ginger, stock, fish sauce, star anise and brown sugar. Bring to a boil, then reduce heat and simmer for 45 minutes.

In the meantime, cook rice noodles according to the instructions on the package. Drain and set aside.

Arrange mung bean sprouts, sprigs of Thai basil, jalapeños and limes on a platter and set on the table.

Use a slotted spoon and remove onions, ginger and star anise from the pot. Add shredded turkey to the pot, and return it to a simmer. Taste the soup and adjust seasoning with additional fish sauce and/or salt, if needed.

Divide rice noodles, cilantro and scallions evenly among large soup bowls, then ladle hot stock over the top, making sure each bowl gets a healthy serving of turkey.

Serve immediately, and serve the garnishes on the side.

Cover and refrigerate leftovers, keeping noodles separate, for up to 3 days.

BOXING DAY LEFTOVERS

DIRECTIONS CONT'D:

Very VERY gently fold about a quarter of the beaten egg whites into the chocolate mixture to lighten it. This is the magic, so go slowly and carefully. Add 1/4 of the beaten egg whites at a time, being sure to fully incorporate before adding more. You want to be sure you don't see any of the whites. Continue to gently fold until the mixture is a lovely shade of milk chocolate, making sure there aren't any white streaks.

Scrape the batter into the pan and smooth the top.

Set the pan on a rimmed baking sheet and bake until the top is puffed and cracked and the center is no longer wobbly, 35 to 40 minutes. Be careful not to bake the cake beyond this point.

Let the cake cool in the pan on a rack. Leave the cake in the springform pan.

The center of the cake will sink as it cools, forming a sort of crater—this is a good thing, so don't worry!

Let the cake cool completely.

If you're making this a day ahead, store the cake at room temperature, keeping it in the springform pan. Do not top with the whipped cream yet! You want to wait to add the whipped cream until right before serving the cake.

To make the whipped cream, whip the cream, confectioners' sugar, and vanilla in a large bowl with a handheld mixer until soft—not stiff—peaks form.

Using a spatula, fill the sunken center of the cake with the whipped cream, swirling the cream to the edges of the crater. Dust the top lightly with cocoa powder.

Run the tip of a knife around the edge of the cake, carefully remove the sides of the pan, and cut into wedges to serve.

Store any leftovers airtight in the refrigerator— if, by some chance, there are any. Whenever I've made this, people are literally liking the plate to get at the last crumbs.

Chocolate Cloud Cake

You'll float away on a cloud of chocolate heaven after one bite of these souffle-ish flourless cake. The recipe is by the late incredible writer and cooking instructor, Richard Sax and is absolutely perfect for all your special occasions.

INGREDIENTS:

- *For the Cake:*
- *8 ounces (225g) best-quality bittersweet chocolate, coarsely chopped (I use Ghirardelli or Schaffenberger)*
- *1/2 cup (110g) unsalted butter, at room temperature and cut into 1-tablespoon pieces*
- *6 large eggs*
- *1 cup (200g) sugar*
- *2 tablespoons cognac or Grand Marnier (you can leave this out, but I highly recommend adding it -- I love using Grand Marnier)*
- *Finely grated zest of 1 orange (about 1 tablespoon -- this part is also optional, but I highly recommend leaving it in)*
- *For the Whipped Cream*
- *1 1/2 cups (355g) heavy cream, very cold*
- *3 tablespoons confectioners' sugar (powdered sugar will keep the whipped cream fluffy -- don't use granulated)*
- *1 teaspoon pure vanilla extract*
- *Unsweetened cocoa powder and/or bitter*

DIRECTIONS:

For the cake:

Heat the oven to 350°F (175°C), and place the rack in the center.

Line the bottom of an 9-inch (20cm) springform pan with parchment paper. (Do NOT butter the pan and parchment.)

Fill a saucepan about 1/4 way with water, and place on stove. Set a heatproof bowl OVER the saucepan, making sure the bottom of the bowl is NOT touching the water.

Add the chocolate to the bowl, and bring the water to a simmer. Gently whisk the chocolate occasionally to help it melt.

When the chocolate is melted, remove bowl from the heat and whisk the butter in until the mixture is lovely and smooth.

Take out 2 small bowls. Separate 4 of the eggs, placing 4 yolks in one bowl and 4 whites in the other bowl.

In a large bowl, whisk 2 whole eggs and the 4 egg yolks with 1/2 cup of the sugar just until combined.

Slowly whisk in the warm chocolate mixture into the egg mixture. And then whisk in the Cognac or Grand Marnier and the orange zest. Set aside.

In the bowl of a stand mixer, beat the 4 egg whites until foamy, about 2 minutes. You can also use a hand mixer, if you don't have a stand mixer.

Gradually add the remaining 1/2 cup sugar and beat until gorgeous glossy, soft peaks form that hold their shape but aren't stiff, about 5 minutes more.

Pear and Goat Cheese Endive Salad

INGREDIENTS:

- 1/4 cup extra-virgin olive oil
- 2 tablespoons balsamic vinegar
- 2 tablespoons walnut oil
- 1 tablespoon finely chopped fresh chives
- salt and freshly ground pepper
- 4 medium endives, cored and cut crosswise into 1-inch pieces
- 2 ounces goat cheese, crumbled (about 2/3 cup)
- 2 pears, thinly sliced
- 1/4 cup chopped walnuts

DIRECTIONS:

Pour vinegar into a bowl. Whisk in the olive oil in a thin stream, then whisk in the walnut oil. Stir in the chives.

Season with salt and pepper. Add the endive and toss to fully coat them.

Sprinkle with goat cheese and arrange 3-4 slices of pear on each plate.

DIRECTIONS CONT'D:

Preheat your oven to 200'c / 400'f /Gas mark 6

Now for the fancy stuff.

With a sharp knife cut the pastry at a 24 'angle move your knife down 1 cm down the pastry and cut again and continue until you have a fringe effect. Repeat on the other side of the pastry.

Now brush the edges of the fringe with a little water and begin the lattice. Fold in the ends of the pastry to encase the end of the wellington, then alternate the cut fringe strips over the top of the cabbage leaves. The wet edges should secure them into place. Decorate with any trimmings that you may have and then brush with your chosen glaze.

Very carefully transfer it to a baking tray with a piece of parchment on it.
Cook for 50 – 60 mins until golden brown, crisp and flaky.

Mushroom Wellington

One of my absolute favourite things to cook for a dinner party is a Beef Wellington, but I always feel guilty about giving a poor substitution for friends who are vegetarians.

Serving this vegetarian Wellington alongside the always goes down well and usually guests have a piece of each!

If you would like your Wellington to be perfect for a vegan appetite, substitute the egg wash for a vegan milk, (coconut, soya, almond) and make sure that your pre made pastry is suitable.

INGREDIENTS:

Serves 6
Ingredients:
200g / 8oz selection of mushrooms, finely sliced
1 onion, finely chopped
1 garlic clove, crushed
2 tablespoon rapeseed oil
200g / 8 oz cashew nuts
100g / 4oz white bread
1 teaspoon dried tarragon or thyme
2 tablespoon of good quality soy sauce
1 teaspoon marmite
1 teaspoon lemon juice
Pinch of sugar
1 savoy cabbage
Salt and freshly ground black pepper
250g / 10oz pack puff pastry
 * Egg to glaze

DIRECTIONS:

Heat 1 tablespoon of the oil in a deep saucepan and when warm add the chopped onion. Fry until soft and translucent and then add your medley of mushrooms and the garlic. Reduce the heat a little and cook out the mushrooms until soft (about 10 mins). Remove from the heat and set aside.

Bring a pan of salted water to the boil. Take about 5 leaves from the savoy cabbage and blanch for a couple of minutes to soften in the boiling water. Transfer to ice cold water to refresh and to keep the crisp green colour. Set aside.

Put the cashews and breadcrumbs into a food processor and blitz to a fine crumb.

In a bowl, bring together the crumb mix the, mushroom mix, tarragon, marmite, soya sauce, pinch of sugar and lemon juice, season. Combine well.

Lay your pastry out on a floured surface. Remove the cabbage leaves from the water and pat dry, place them down the centre of the pastry. Carefully place the mushroom mix down the centre of the cabbage leaves.

Wrap the leaves around the mushrooms neatly.

Pumpkin Cumin Fritters with Yogurt Dip

Great party food, or just chilling with the family in front of a Christmas film. It looks like a lot of ingredients, but the fitters are quite simple and quick to make. Substitute the pumpkin with courgette or a mix of other vegetables, if not a pumpkin fan

Make the dipping sauce in advance and keep refrigerated

INGREDIENTS:

- **500g/1lb pumpkin flesh grated**
- **1 tablespoon cumin seeds**
- **3 spring onions**
- **1 red chilli – finely chopped**
- **1 large teaspoon grated fresh ginger**
- **1 large teaspoon finely chopped lemongrass**
- **2 lime leaves, finely chopped or the grated rind of the lime to be used in the dip**
- **¼ teaspoon ground coriander**
- **1 tablespoon soya sauce**
- **Pinch of sugar**
- **50g / 2 oz plain flour**
- **50g / 2oz cornflour**
- **Salt & pepper**
- **Fresh herbs:**
- **1 heaped tablespoon fresh coriander**
- **1 heaped tablespoon fresh basil**
- **Oil (vegetable)**
- **Yogurt Dip**
- **250g/8oz pot natural full fat yogurt.**
- **2 tablespoons of good quality mango chutney**
- **1 lime, juiced**
- **1 red chilli finely chopped**
- **1 x large handful coriander**
- **Pinch salt**

DIRECTIONS:

Combine all of the fritter ingredients together in a bowl until lovely and sticky. If the mix is too dry to bind, and a little water, but be patient.

Heat the oil in a deep frying pan until hot and then drop the heat down a little.

Make a fritter into a patty shape. Use a tablespoon to add a fritter to the hot oil. Do not overcrowd the pan and use a slotted spoon to turn the fritters so that they cook evenly. Cooking time will depend upon oil temperature and the size of the fritter. I usually allow about 8 minutes, but if you are not sure, split one to check.

Once golden brown & Crispy, remove from the oil and place on kitchen paper to absorb excess oil. Start the next batch and continue until all cooked.

Serve hot.
(For Gluten free, substitute plain flour for rice flour)

For Yogurt Dip:
Combine the yogurt, mango chutney, coriander and a healthy squeeze of lime. Chill until needed.

CHRISTMAS VEGETARIAN FEAST

Brandy Butter

This makes a great gift, especially when it is accompanied by a box full of mince pies! Pop it on the table with your Christmas Pudding. A little goes a long way.

INGREDIENTS:

- **125g /5oz unsalted butter (room temperature)**
- **125g /5oz soft light brown sugar**
- **6 tablespoons brandy**

DIRECTIONS:

Place the butter in a bowl and beat with a wooden spoon until soft. Gradually add the sugar to the butter, beating after each addition so that the mixture remains smooth.

Finally you will have a light and fluffy mixture.

Beat in the brandy a spoonful at a time. When all combined, transfer to the serving dish and refrigerate until needed.

Egg Nog

Have a pitcher in your fridge ready to serve to friends who drop by, while you're decking the halls, opening gifts, or any time you want a festive drink.

INGREDIENTS:

- *4 egg yolks*
- *1/3 cup sugar, plus 1 tablespoon*
- *1 pint whole milk*
- *1 cup heavy cream*
- *3 ounces bourbon*
- *1 teaspoon freshly grated nutmeg*
- *4 egg whites*

DIRECTIONS:

In the bowl of a stand mixer, beat the egg yolks until they lighten in color. Gradually add the 1/3 cup sugar and continue to beat until it is completely dissolved.

Add the milk, cream, bourbon and nutmeg and stir to combine.

Place the egg whites in the bowl of a stand mixer and beat to soft peaks. With the mixer still running gradually add the 1 tablespoon of sugar and beat until stiff peaks form.

Whisk the egg whites into the mixture. Chill and serve.

In the bowl of a stand mixer, beat the egg yolks until they lighten in color. Gradually add the 1/3 cup sugar and continue to beat until it is completely dissolved. Set aside.

In a medium saucepan, over high heat, combine the milk, heavy cream and nutmeg and bring just to a boil, stirring occasionally.

Remove from the heat and gradually temper the hot mixture into the egg and sugar mixture. Then return everything to the pot and cook until the mixture reaches 160 degrees F.

Remove from the heat, stir in the bourbon, pour into a medium mixing bowl, and set in the refrigerator to chill.

In a medium mixing bowl, beat the egg whites to soft peaks. With the mixer running gradually add the 1 tablespoon of sugar and beat until stiff peaks form. Whisk the egg whites into the chilled mixture.

DIRECTIONS CONT'D:

For the Crust: Sift the flour and salt together and add to bowl of food processor.

Add the butter and pulse a few times until the butter resembles tiny pebbles.

With the motor running, add the ice water, 1 tablespoon at a time. Add enough water to make the dough just barely come together. It will still look loose and crumbly, but you will know it's enough water when you can take a small pinch of the dough and it just holds together.

When the dough is ready, turn it out onto a couple of sheets of plastic wrap. Wrap the plastic wrap around the dough, and, using the plastic wrap, create a ball. Flatten it out with your hands a bit, and then refrigerate while you make the filling.

For the Filling: In a small saucepan over medium low heat, melt the butter. Stir in the sugar and vinegar and bring mixture to a boil. Place eggs in a mixing bowl and beat well. I usually use my stand mixer for this step, but you can also use a hand mixer. Add a few tablespoons of the sugar mixture to the eggs, to temper the eggs, and mix for a couple of minutes. This will ensure you don't get scrambled eggs.

Add the rest of the sugar mixture to the eggs and beat well to incorporate all the ingredients. Add the vanilla and beat for another few seconds.

Chess Pie

My aunt made this every year and it's the best pecan pie you'll ever have! Loads of pecans, and the filling doesn't have corn syrup which makes it sweeter and richer. It will make the end of any holiday meal extra sweet. A little piece goes a long way!

INGREDIENTS:

- *Serves 8*

- *Pie Crust Ingredients*
- *1 ½ cups sifted all-purpose flour (measure and then sift)*
- *½ teaspoon salt*
- *½ cup cold butter, cut into small pieces*
- *2-4 tablespoons ice water*
- *Filling Ingredients*
- *½ cup butter*
- *1 ½ cups granulated sugar*
- *1 tablespoon apple cider vinegar (do NOT use white wine vinegar. You can substitute white vinegar, but apple cider really is the best)*
- *3 eggs*
- *1 teaspoon vanilla extract*
- *Pinch of salt*
- *¾ cup coarsely chopped pecans*

DIRECTIONS:

For the Crust: Sift the flour and salt together and add to bowl of food processor.

Add the butter and pulse a few times until the butter resembles tiny pebbles.

With the motor running, add the ice water, 1 tablespoon at a time. Add enough water to make the dough just barely come together. It will still look loose and crumbly, but you will know it's enough water when you can take a small pinch of the dough and it just holds together.

When the dough is ready, turn it out onto a couple of sheets of plastic wrap. Wrap the plastic wrap around the dough, and, using the plastic wrap, create a ball. Flatten it out with your hands a bit, and then refrigerate while you make the filling.

For the Filling: In a small saucepan over medium low heat, melt the butter. Stir in the sugar and vinegar and bring mixture to a boil. Place eggs in a mixing bowl and beat well. I usually use my stand mixer for this step, but you can also use a hand mixer. Add a few tablespoons of the sugar mixture to the eggs, to temper the eggs, and mix for a couple of minutes. This will ensure you don't get scrambled eggs.

Add the rest of the sugar mixture to the eggs and beat well to incorporate all the ingredients. Add the vanilla and beat for another few seconds.

INGREDIENTS:

- **150 g raisins**
- **150 g sultanas**
- **150g currants**
- **25g glace cherries cut up**
- **25g chopped prunes or figs**
- **200ml Brandy, Rum or your favoured tipple**
- **1 lemon – finely grated zest**
- **1 clementine – finely grated zest**
- **125g plain flour**
- **150g vegetarian suet**
- **125g breadcrumbs**
- **170g dark soft brown sugar**
- **1 large Bramley apple peeled, cored and grated**
- **3 x large eggs,**
- **1 teaspoon baking powder**
- **1 teaspoon ground cinnamon**
- **1 teaspoon ground mixed spice**
- **¼ teaspoon ground cloves**
- **Butter for greasing**
- **100ml whisky or brandy for flaming your pudding.**
- **3 pint pudding basin or Christmas pudding sphere tin,**
- **Baking parchment & foil**

DIRECTIONS:

A couple of days before Stir It Up Sunday, put all of the dried fruit in a bowl with the alcohol, cover and leave to soak for a couple of days if possible. (The longer the better).

In a large bowl, combine all of the ingredients and then add the fruit and all of the lovely juices.

Now is the time to make your wishes.

Put some water into a steamer and bring to a simmer. If you don't have a steamer, use a large heavy based saucepan with an upturned saucer in the base.

Grease the pudding basin and lid and put all of the pudding mix into the basin. Make sure to scrape all of the goodness out of the mixing bowl. Place a round disk of parchment onto the top of the pudding mix and then make sure that the lid is firmly on. If you have no lid, use a triple layer of parchment and tie tightly with string. I use the string to make a handle as well. Then cover with foil.

Place in the steamer and steam slowly for 5 hours. Check regularly, that the water does not boil dry.

Take you pudding out and leave to cool. Re wrap with clean foil and parchment if used and set safely aside to mature.

On Christmas day, put the pudding in the steamer once again and steam for a further three hours.

Turn out onto a serving plate. If you are intending to flame your pudding, make sure that it is one with a lip, so that the liquid doesn't run off.

Get your matches ready. Heat about 100ml brandy or whisky in a small saucepan. Do not boil or you will cook off the alcohol. When hot pour over the pudding and light.

Parade your pudding to the table.

Great served with Lisa's eggnog! (page 89)

Jane's Christmas Pudding

Stir-Up Sunday is a great family tradition. It is the day when the Christmas Pudding is made and it is always the last Sunday before the start of advent, which gives the pudding just enough time to mature nicely.

Obviously there is a lot of stirring that goes into making the pudding, but the name originally comes from " Stir up we beseech thee O Lord" the beginning of the collect for the day in the Book of Common Prayer.

It has been a tradition for many years, created by the Victorians, like so many of our Christmas festivities. We take it in turns to stir the pudding and of course, make a wish. I also still like to put charms or silver sixpences in the pudding, but to be on the safe side, I wrap them in some parchment.

Even the flaming of the pudding is steeped in tradition with a nod to the pagan ritual of celebrating the winter solstice and bringing warmth and light into the darkness of the winter day.

Plan ahead and make sure that you soak the fruit for at least 24 - 48 hours. Christmas Pudding is a great way to use up all of the bits of dried fruit that accumulate in the kitchen cupboard. The ingredients below are just for guidance, just go with the flow. I've been known to bung in the odd chopped dried apricot, figs, prunes, even mango! Talk about living on the wild side.

Christmas music is not mandatory, but fun.

DIRECTIONS:

When potatoes are cooked, carefully drain them in the colander.

Remove the cheesecloth or tea infuser. If you didn't use a tea infuser or cheesecloth, carefully remove the garlic and rosemary sprigs. Don't worry about removing the thyme (if you used it)- - the leaves are so small they will incorporate just fine into the mashed potatoes.

Using a ricer, rice the potatoes and put them back in their original pot.

I usually place the ricer in the large pot and use a large spoon to transfer spoonfuls of potatoes from colander to ricer. You will need to do this several times, but it's SO worth it to get gorgeous fluffy mashed potatoes.

Take the flavored cream and add it back to the pot with the potatoes about 1/2 cup at a time.

Stir in butter, 2 tablespoons at a time.

Keep adding cream and butter, stirring over low heat, until the potatoes are the consistency you like.

You WILL have extra cream. Save it to use when reheating the potatoes the next day.

Serve immediately, or store in your fridge.

Truffle Mashed Potatoes

Once you cook your potatoes in cream, I promise you'll never go back to water. The cream is full of flavor, thanks to the herbs, and the starchy flavor of the potatoes adds another level of flavor.

INGREDIENTS:

- **4 pounds Yukon potatoes (the golden ones), peeled and cut into quarters**
- **1 bay leaf**
- **1-2 sprigs fresh rosemary**
- **1-2 sprigs fresh thyme, optional**
- **1 clove garlic, peeled**
- **Kosher salt and freshly ground black pepper**
- **Heavy cream (I always buy the 32 ounce size -- you won't use all of it, but there will be extra to use in other recipes)**
- **1 stick unsalted butter (use European for extra creaminess)**
- **1 - 4 tablespoons Truffle butter (totally depends on how much truffle flavor you want!)**
- **Helpful kitchen tools**
- **cheesecloth or tea infuser**
- **ricer**

DIRECTIONS:

DO THE DAY BEFORE:

If you want to get a head start -- peel and cut your potatoes the day before. Place them a large bowl, cover with water and store in your fridge. This will prevent them from browning. Before cooking, drain them in a colander placed in your sink, give them a quick rinse and then place them in a large pot.

Place potatoes in large pot.

In a cheesecloth or tea infuser, place the bay leaf, garlic, rosemary and thyme. If you don't have either, add the aromatics directly to the pot with the potatoes.

Cover the potatoes with the cream. You want the cream to just barely cover the potatoes.
To prevent the cream from overflowing, don't cover the pot.

Cook over medium heat, at a gentle simmer (just a few bubbles here and there), until potatoes are cooked through. This should take about 10-15 minutes.

BE SURE YOU COOK AT A GENTLE SIMMER AND NOT A BOIL. IF THE CREAM BOILS IT'S LIKELY TO OVERFLOW AND CREATE A HUGE MESS.

Place a colander over a bowl in your sink. DON'T FORGET TO PUT A BOWL UNDER THE COLANDER TO CATCH THE CREAM.

Hasselback Butternut Squash

I LOVE butternut squash. My family, not so much. So I try ENDLESS recipes hoping one will get them to love it as much as I do. And this was that one!

INGREDIENTS:

- *2 medium butternut squash*
- *4 tablespoons extra virgin olive oil*
- *kosher salt and black pepper*
- *8 tablespoons unsalted butter, at room temperature*
- *3 tablespoons maple syrup*
- *2 teaspoons chopped fresh rosemary*
- *1/4 cup pomegranate seeds*
- *1/2 cup walnuts, toasted and roughly chopped*

DIRECTIONS:

Preheat your oven to 425 degrees F/218 C.

With a sharp knife, cut the squash in half lengthwise and scoop out the seeds with a large spoon or ice cream scoop. Place the squash, cut side down, on your cutting board and remove the skin with a vegetable peeler.

Rub the inside of the squash with 2 tablespoons olive oil, and season generously with salt and pepper. Place squash cut side down on a large rimmed baking sheet. Roast until the squash begins to soften, about 15-20 minutes.

DIRECTIONS CONT'D:

Meanwhile, in a small bowl, mash together the butter, maple syrup, and chopped rosemary with the back of a fork until combined.

When the squash is finished, transfer to a cutting board, and place it horizontal on the board.

Using a sharp knife, slice through the rounded sides of squash halves, crosswise, going as deep as possible but without cutting all the way through. To make this easier, get 2 wooden spoons (use spoons you don't care about nicking about), and place 1 spoon on either side of the squash to help prevent cutting all the way through.

Return the squash to the baking sheet, scored sides up.

Use a spatula to spread half the maple butter over the squash, making sure to get it into the slices. Season with salt and pepper.

Roast the squash for 30 minutes, remove from oven and spread with the remaining maple butter, spooning any melted butter in the pan over the squash. Return to the oven and roast another 15-20 minutes, until the squash is tender.

Remove the squash from the oven and transfer to a serving plate. I love the garnish the platter with extra sprigs of fresh rosemary.

Drizzle over any maple butter left on the pan and sprinkle with pomegranate seeds and toasted walnuts.

Serve warm!

Leg of Lamb

My godmother was French and this is her recipe. Every time I make it i know she's looking over my shoulder, reminding me to season it with love......and an extra splash of wine!

INGREDIENTS:

- **6 garlic cloves, minced**
- **1 tablespoon chopped fresh rosemary leaves**
- **1 tablespoon chopped thyme**
- **1 tablespoon dry mustard**
- **Kosher salt**
- **Freshly ground black pepper**
- **5 tablespoons butter, softened**
- **1 (6-pound) bone in leg of lamb**
- **4 to 5 pounds small unpeeled potatoes (16 to 20 potatoes) -- red or yellow**
- **zest of 3 large lemons**
- **2 tablespoons extra virgin olive oil**

DIRECTIONS:

Preheat oven to 400 degrees F/200 degrees C

With a paring knife, score the top of the leg of lamb. The top of the leg is where the fat is, so you'll be scoring through the fat. Use the knife to make shallow cuts into the meat, in a criss cross pattern.

In a small bowl, mix together the garlic, rosemary, thyme, dry mustard, 1 teaspoon salt and 1/2 teaspoon pepper.

Add the butter and use a fork to create a butter paste.

Place the lamb, scored side up, on a rack and place the rack in a large roasting pan.

In a bowl, toss the potatoes with the olive oil and lemon zest.

Add the potatoes to the bottom of the roasting pan.

Roast the lamb for 20 minutes, then turn the heat down to 350 degrees F and roast for another 1 to 1 1/4 hours, until the meat reaches 135 degrees.

Remove from oven and let the lamb rest for 15 minutes before serving.

FOODIES NOTES:

You can also make this with boneless lamb, but you'll need to adjust cooking time. It's really important to know the temperature of your oven, so you don't overcook the lamb. Cook it for less time if you're not sure because you can always cook it longer, if needed

Caramelized Banana Shallots

This onion side dish is so delicious, one of my absolute favourites! Great with any roast, including Nut Roast!

INGREDIENTS:

- *Serves 4*
- *4 Medium banana shallots*
- *40g / 3.5oz unsalted butter*
- *200ml chicken stock*
- *25g / 1oz Light soft brown sugar*
- *Pinch of sea salt.*

DIRECTIONS:

Trim the roots, but leave base attached to the shallot and carefully peel away the outer skins, so that the shallot is still whole. Now cut the shallot in half lengthwise.

Pop the butter into a frying pan (perfect if it is an oven proof one) and over a high heat melt the butter until it start to foam.

Place the shallots into the hot butter, presentation side down and allow to turn light brown.

Add the stock & the sugar. Reduce to create a delicious sticky syrup.

Transfer the shallots to a baking tray (if your saucepan is not ovenproof), and cook in a hot oven at 200'c 400'f until fully cooked, soft, caramelised and unctuous!

Season and serve.

Bromyard is known for its festivals, but the Christmas Lights are without doubt, my favourite! It brings the community together but also masses of people make a special journey to see them!

The team "The Light Brigade" are entirely made of volunteers who build and erect the Christmas lights every year. The group has been in operation for nearly sixty years and its members are from all walks of life Every new addition to the display is built by hand, in Bromyard. All share the same passion of making Bromyard shine at Christmas!

Thank you "Light Brigade"!

Brussels Sprouts with Chestnuts

INGREDIENTS:

- *Serves 4 sprout lovers (8 non sprout lovers)*
- *Ingredients:*
- *500g / 1 lb chestnuts*
- *500ml / 1 pint turkey or chicken stock*
- *1 kilo / 2 lb Brussel Sprouts*
- *75g / 3 oz unsalted butter*
- *Black pepper*

DIRECTIONS:

Pre heat your oven to 180'c 350'f Gas mark 4.

Cut a nick in the skin of each chestnut and put in a large saucepan of cold water. Bring to the boil, remove from the heat and peel off the shell & skin from the chestnuts. As soon as this becomes tricky, return the pan to the heat and bring to the boil again.

Of course, you could use pre peeled chestnuts, but where is the fun in that?

Put the chestnuts into a casserole dish, add the stock. Cook in the oven for about 30 minutes until the chestnuts are tender.

Meanwhile, put the sprouts into a saucepan with salted water, bring to the boil and simmer for about 10 minutes so that they are cooked but still crunchy. Drain

Heat the butter in a saucepan, then add both sprouts and chestnuts. Turn until the sprouts are just beginning to brown.

Season and turn into your serving dish
For an extra something fry off some crispy lardons of bacon first before frying sprouts and chestnuts. Sprinkle on top of the finished dish.

For vegetarian, substitute chicken stock for vegetable stock.

Brandy Gravy

This gravy is SO good you'll want to drink it......but, trust me, it's even better poured over your turkey, or your mashed potatoes.....or both!

INGREDIENTS:

- **1 stick unsalted butter**
- **1 1/2 cups chopped yellow onion**
- **1/4 cup flour**
- **1 teaspoon salt**
- **1/2 teaspoon freshly ground black pepper**
- **turkey drippings plus chicken stock to make 2 cups, heated**
- **1 tablespoon Cognac or brandy**
- **1 tablespoon white wine**
- **1 tablespoon heavy cream**

DIRECTIONS:

In a large sauté pan, cook the butter and onions over medium-low heat for 12 to 15 minutes, until the onions are lightly browned. You want to make sure the onions are lightly browned...this adds the most wonderful caramelized flavor to the gravy.

Sprinkle flour into the pan, whisk to incorporate the flour with the onions, and then season with the salt and pepper. Cook for 2 to 3 minutes.

Add the warm turkey drippings/stock mixture and Cognac, and cook uncovered for 4 to 5 minutes until thickened.
Add the wine and cream and cook for another 1 -2 minutes.

Season, to taste, and serve.

Herb Roasted Turkey

If you're a traditionalist, like my dad, and love your turkey for Thanksgiving AND Christmas, then you'll love this recipe. Yes, there are a lot of ingredients, but it's not a complicated dish and the flavor is off the charts delicious!

INGREDIENTS:

- **Serves 12 -15**
- **Time: 5 hours**
- **one 15 lb turkey**
- **4 tablespoons olive oil**
- **1 stick of butter, softened**
- **6 cloves, minced garlic**
- **4 teaspoons fresh squeezed lemon juice**
- **4 teaspoons Coleman's dry mustard**
- **2 tablespoons fresh rosemary, finely chopped**
- **2 tablespoons fresh tarragon, finely chopped**
- **2 teaspoons fresh thyme, leaves finely chopped**
- **3 teaspoons salt**
- **1 teaspoon pepper**
- **2 cups white wine (I recommend having 2 bottles on stand by)**

DIRECTIONS:

Preheat oven to 325 degrees F/ 165 C. Place turkey on roasting rack in a large roasting pan, breast side up.

In a small bowl, mix olive oil, butter, garlic, lemon juice, mustard, herbs and salt and pepper. With your hands (gloves will come in handy here), massage about 1/2 the mixture evenly all over the turkey.

Carefully lift up the skin (*you don't want to rip it, so gently slide your finger between the skin and the meat to loosen it*) and add the rest of the mixture under the skin. Focus on the breast, and legs --- this will create even MORE flavor. Pour the wine into the bottom of the roasting pan.

Roast the turkey until the skin is golden brown, about 4 hours, or until a thermometer registers 160 degrees. If the skin starts getting too brown before the turkey is finished, cover loosely with foil.

VERY IMPORTANT: Keep an eye on the wine level! I usually take a peek every 15-20 minutes.

If the wine starts to evaporate add another 2 cups of wine. Depending on the size of your turkey, you may go through an entire bottle, or 2 of wine. That's ok!! The wine keeps the meat nice and moist, plus adds flavor!

Remove from oven and rest the turkey for about 15-30 minutes.

CHRISTMAS FEAST

The Key Word

This one is quick but not s easy as it sounds!

Each player has a piece of paper and pencil. Take it in turn to call out a three letter word. Players have three minutes to write down as many words that contain the "Key" word.

For example:
"TIP"
antipathy.
multiplex.
stipulate.
multiport.
fingertip.
centipede.
antipodes.
antipasto.

the cinnamon puffs are the perfect "game snack" to nibble on while your drink your morning coffee on Christmas morning (cinnamon puffs, page 66)

Bucks Fizz

INGREDIENTS:

- *makes 4*
- *1 bottle Champagne*
- *1 cup freshly squeezed orange juice*

DIRECTIONS:

Pour 2 ounces of orange juice into each champagne flute.

Top off with champagne.

Bucks Fizz is the simplest of drinks to make, but perfect with your decadent scrambled egg with smoked salmon. A non-alcoholic alternative would be a St. Clements, orange juice and bitter lemon.

Here are some suggestions from team Foodie, for a bit of light entertainment during Christmas Day!

"Keep a straight face"

Divide your guests who are sitting at the table into two teams. They need to be facing each other. The objective for the first team is to make the second team crack and laugh. Use cracker jokes, funny faces, performances etc all allowed – BUT NO physical contact i.e tickles!
Your team is out when the last person cracks a smile. Time yourselves and see who is the winning team . Have some lovely chocolates on standby for the winning team.

& the band played on

Warning – this one can get a little noisy, but if you get a couple of competitive guests, it can be huge fun.

In advance gather together and give to each team:

- Empty milk or wine bottles
- A Jug of water
- Spoons
- Rubber bands
- Rulers / combs
- Tissue paper

Give each team 5 minutes to create instruments and 5 minutes to plan and rehearse. They then put on their performance. Have some really cheesy things to offer the winning team like kazoos, penny whistles. If they win, they can use these in their next performance.   Yup, it's going to get noisy!

DIRECTIONS CONT'D:

Spoon into prepared muffin cups, filling only 3/4 of the way. (I filled mine higher and they ended up spilling over a bit and doming less than they are capable of.) Bake miniature muffins for about 12 to 14 minutes. When finished, muffins will feel springy to the touch and a tester inserted into the center will come out clean. Transfer them in their pan to a wire rack.

As soon as you feel you're able to pick one up, but when they're still warm, take your first puff and dip it in the browned butter so the butter coats all sides of the puff.

Don't be afraid to pick up the browned butter solids at the bottom of the saucepan; they're the dreamiest part. Let any excess butter drip off for a second before gently rolling the butter-soaked cake top in cinnamon-sugar. I find if you roll too firmly, or have too much wet/not absorbed butter on top, the sugar can clump off, which is heartbreaking.

Transfer puff to wire rack to set and repeat with remaining puffs. Eat warm.

Cinnamon Puffs

INGREDIENTS:

- *2/3 cup granulated sugar*
- *1 tablespoon ground cinnamon*
- *8 tablespoons unsalted butter*
- *PUFFS*
- *1 1/2 cups all-purpose flour*
- *1 1/2 teaspoons baking powder*
- *1/2 teaspoon baking soda*
- *1/2 teaspoon table salt*
- *1/4 teaspoon freshly grated nutmeg*
- *1/2 cup granulated sugar*
- *1/3 cup (5 tablespoons plus 1 teaspoon) unsalted butter, at room temperature, plus extra for greasing muffin cups*
- *1 large egg*
- *1 teaspoon pure vanilla extract*
- *1/2 cup buttermilk (if you don't have buttermilk, use regular milk instead but don't add the baking soda)*

DIRECTIONS:

Preheat oven to 350°F. Butter 30 miniature muffin cups, or line cups with paper liners.

Prepare coatings: In a small saucepan, melt 8 tablespoons butter over medium heat and continue to cook it, stirring frequently, until lovely golden brown bits form on the bottom. It will smell nutty and heavenly. Immediately remove from heat and set aside. In a small bowl, combine 2/3 cup sugar and cinnamon. Set aside as well.

You definitely want to prepare the browned butter and cinnamon sugar FIRST, so you can dip and roll the puffs when they're warm out of the oven.

Prepare puffs: Whisk flour, baking powder, baking soda, salt and nutmeg together in a medium bowl and set aside. In the large bowl of an electric mixer, beat softened butter and sugar together until light and fluffy. Add egg and vanilla and beat until combined. Mix in 1/3 of flour mixture, followed by 1/2 of buttermilk, repeating again and finishing with the flour mixture. Mix only until combined.

The Best Ever Coffee Cake

This recipe is an old one and a REALLY good one! It goes back 21 years to when I was part of a playgroup. We'd meet up at each other's houses, the kids would play, and we'd chat about our kids while drinking vats of coffee and this insanely delicious coffee cake. Bonus - the recipe makes 2!!

INGREDIENTS:

- **1 Box Duncan Hines yellow cake mix (I use the deluxe moist one)**
- **1 small box Instant vanilla pudding**
- **4 eggs**
- **3/4 cup vegetable oil**
- **3/4 cup water**
- **2 tsp vanilla**
- **1/2 cup sugar**
- **1/2 cup light brown sugar**
- **2 Tbsp cinnamon**
- **1/2 cup chopped pecans**
- **For the Icing:**
- **1 1/2 cup powdered sugar**
- **1 tsp vanilla**
- **1/4 cup whole milk**

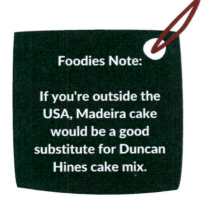

Foodies Note:

If you're outside the USA, Madeira cake would be a good substitute for Duncan Hines cake mix.

DIRECTIONS:

Preheat oven to 350 degrees.

In a standing mixer mix the first 6 ingredients for about 5-8 minutes. You want them to be extremely well blended!

While the batter is mixing, prepare the cake pans and the nut/sugar mixture.

In a separate bowl, combine the 2 sugars, cinnamon and pecans. Set aside.

Grease and flour 2 round or square cake pans.

To assemble the coffee cake:

Put 1/3 sugar mixture into bottom of each pan.

Divide 1/2 cake batter between each pan. Then sprinkle 1/3 sugar mixture over cake batter in each pan. Add the rest of the cake batter to each pan. Top each pan with remaining sugar mixture. Take a knife and swirl through cake and sugar mixtures to make it look like marble.

Bake for about 30-35 minutes. Test by inserting a toothpick into the center. They are done when the toothpick comes out clean, or with a few crumbs.

Cool the cakes thoroughly on a wire rack before icing them.

For the icing: In a small bowl whisk together the sugar, vanilla and milk.

Drizzle icing over cooled cakes.

Avocado and Goat Cheese on Toast

This is such a favourite. I swap and change the toppings. I sometimes add pancetta crumb, or a poached egg. A drizzle of chilli jam is also a delicious addition.

INGREDIENTS:

- **2 ripe avocados**
- **Juice of half a lime**
- **½ red chilli (seeds removed and finely chopped).**
- **2 tsp of flat leaf parsley**
- **Fresh dill**
- **Freshly ground black pepper & Sea salt**
- **Soft goats cheese**
- **Crusty granary bread sliced & salted butter**
- **Drizzle of olive oil**

DIRECTIONS:

Cut the avocado in half and remove the stone. Peel and cut into small chunks.

Pop into a bowl with the lime juice, chilli, a pinch of the seasoning, pepper and parsley.

Toast the granary bread but if it is fresh I would have it as it is. Butter and divide the avocado mix between the slices.

Crush the goats cheese gently and add a teaspoon full to the avocado.

Drizzle a small amount of olive, season and sprinkle with dill.

Serve and enjoy.

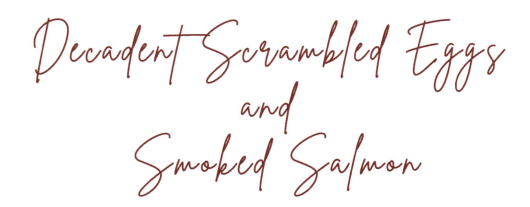

Decadent Scrambled Eggs and Smoked Salmon

The perfect breakfast for Christmas morning! Investing in some fantastic artisan cured salmon is a great treat.

INGREDIENTS:

- *40 ml double cream*
- *20g butter*
- *Myrtle's dill seasoning or a pinch of seasalt and dill*
- *Freshly ground black pepper*
- *4 free range eggs*
- *125g smoked salmon*
- *Chopped chives to taste*
- *Toasted sourdough and a little additional butter*

DIRECTIONS:

Put the cream into a heavy based pan and bring to the boil. Add the butter and heat until foamy.

Reduce the heat to low and season.

Beat the eggs and add to the cream mix.

Stir the mix until softly set. Don't overcook, reduce to a really low temperature, or even take off the heat and allow the residual heat to continue to cook the mix.

Arrange the smoked salmon in a nest on your serving plates and put the scrambled egg in the centre.

Garnish with chopped chives and a small sprinkling of the dill seasoning.

Toast the bread and butter and all that is left is to eat.

COZY CHRISTMAS MORNING BREAKFAST

Champagne Aperol Spritz

Who doesn't love a little sparkly drink to celebrate the night before Christmas? If you like a little bit of a bitter drink, Campari would be a great substitution.

INGREDIENTS:

- *a bottle of champagne*
- *a bottle of Aperol*
- *Fever Tree club soda*

DIRECTIONS:

Take out 4 of your fanciest champagne flutes. It's Christmas Eve after all, so time for your good crystal.

Fill each champagne glass 2/3 of the way with champagne, then add a splash of Aperol and top off with a splash of club soda.

Hazelnut Meringue

This is my go to for a great dinner party dessert. I discovered it when I was about 12 years old, before I could spell hazelnut or meringue! Handwritten in my first recipe journal, I have such fond memories of this sticky delicious pudding as it was a favourite of my late mothers'.

INGREDIENTS:

- **4 egg whites**
- **9oz / 225g caster sugar**
- **3 – 4 drops of vanilla essence**
- **½ teaspoon vinegar**
- **4 oz / 100g hazelnuts – toasted, skin rubbed off and ground.**
- **½ pint double cream.**
- **Icing sugar for dusting**
- **6oz / 150g raspberries (fresh or frozen)**
- **Butter & cornflour for greasing and lining tins.**
- **2 x 8" sandwich cake tins**
- **Cooking parchment**

DIRECTIONS:

Butter the sandwich tins and then sprinkle some flour in and agitate around the tin so that it sticks to the butter. Put a disc of cooking parchment into the base of each tin.

Set the oven to 375 f / 190'c / Gas mark 5.

Whisk the egg whites until stiff with a rotary whisk. Add the sugar gradually, 1 tablespoon at a time and continue until the mixture is stiff and stands in stiff peaks. Whisk in the vinegar & vanilla and then carefully fold in the ground hazelnuts.

Divide the mixture evenly between the two cake tins and smooth the top with a palette knife. Bake for 30-40 mins, BUT NO LONGER. The top of the meringue will be crisp but the inside will be like soft marshmallow.

Carefully turn onto cooling trays. Do not be concerned if the crisp top cracks.

Whisk the cream and add a drop or two of vanilla. Set some aside for decoration.

Pick out some nice raspberries to decorate the top, set to one side. Fold the remaining raspberries through the cream. Use the cream mix to sandwich the two meringues together. Decorate the top with swirls of cream topped with raspberries.

Before serving, dust with icing sugar.

Rocket & Chicory Salad with Ricotta and Tangerine.

A lovely light salad with great textures. It's a salad that you could eat by itself, but it really works with the Boxing Day ham!

INGREDIENTS:

- *1 x bag rocket, washed*
- *2 x chicory heads shredded*
- *1 x 250g tub ricotta*
- *50 g / 2oz toasted walnuts*
- *2 x tangerine*
- *2 tablespoon Olive Oil*

DIRECTIONS:

Combine the chicory and rocket in a bowl together and keep refrigerated.

Make the dressing. Finely grate the tangerine zest . Juice the tangerines and pour into a small saucepan, simmer until the juice has reduced by half. Combine the zest, juice, oil and vinegar and chill.

When ready to serve, add the walnuts to the bowl of leaves and add dots of the ricotta over the surface.

Drizzle over the dressing and serve.

Paella

One of my family's favorite traditions is Christmas Eve with one of my best friends, her dad and her kids. She's gluten free, so the main course is always paella. My hubby is allergic to mollusks, but if you love mussels, clams and scallops feel free to add them!

INGREDIENTS:

- *Serves 6*
- *1/4 cup extra virgin olive oil*
- *4 ounces ground chorizo, casings removed (you can also use sliced)*
- *1 yellow onion, diced*
- *2 garlic cloves, minced*
- *1 red bell pepper, diced, seeds and pith removed*
- *One 15 ounce can diced tomatoes with juices*
- *1 teaspoon smoked paprika*
- *1-2 good pinches fresh saffron threads*
- *salt*
- *pepper*
- *1 cup white wine*
- *4 cups short grain rice (Bomba or Calasparra)*
- *6 cups chicken stock*
- *8 boneless, skinless chicken thighs*
- *1 pound shrimp, peeled and deveined*
- *2 large handfuls fresh Italian flat leaf parsley*
- *2 lemons, quartered*

DIRECTIONS:

Paella is the name of the pan you cook this dish in, but a large wide shallow heavy bottomed skillet will also work!

Heat oil over medium heat and brown the chicken on both sides. Remove and set aside.

Add chorizo, onion, garlic, red bell pepper, and, stirring often, sauté until the veggies soften and start to glisten. Add the can of tomatoes, paprika, saffron and season with salt and pepper. Give the mixture a stir and cook over low to medium low heat.

The mixture is called "sofrito" and gives the paella it's depth of smokey flavor. You want to cook the mixture until the tomatoes start to caramelize, about 20-30 minutes. The longer it cooks, the more flavor!

Stir in the rice and, similar to risotto, stir the rice for 5 minutes to "toast" it.

Add the wine and simmer for about 5 minutes until the wine evaporates.

Add the chicken broth and give it a quick stir, but then no more stirring!

Add the chicken and, if you love saffron, add and additional pinch of saffron.

Let the mixture cook over medium heat for about 15-20 minutes. Then add the shrimp. The shrimp takes about 8 minutes to cook.

Garnish with parsley and lemon wedges.

This is a fun dish to serve at your table, but be sure you have a table protector so the pan doesn't leave a mark on your table.

CHRISTMAS EVE

INGREDIENTS CONT'D:

- *100g / 4oz dried mixed fruit*
- *75g / 3oz mixed peel*
- *100g / 4oz suet*
- *100g / 4oz dark brown muscavado sugar*
- *100g / 4oz currants*
- *1/2 tsp ground cinnamon*
- *1/2 tsp freshly grated nutmeg*
- *1 tsp mixed spice*
- *1/2 tsp ground ginger*
- *50ml / 2fl oz brandy*
- *50ml / 2fl oz sherry*
- *For the orange pastry*
- *500g / 1lb plain flour*
- *1 tsp baking powder*
- *125g / 5oz unsalted butter, plus extra for greasing*
- *1 tbsp caster sugar*
- *140ml / 5fl oz orange juice*
- *2 oranges, zest only*
- *1 free-range egg, beaten*
- *whipped cream, brandy butter or ice cream, to serve*

DIRECTIONS CONT'D:

Blend the flour, baking powder, salt and butter in a food processor until the mixture resembles breadcrumbs.

Acd the orange zest and blend until well combined, then gradually add the orange juice, blending continuously, until the mixture comes together as a dough.

Turn out the dough onto a lightly floured work surface, knead lightly until smooth, then wrap in cling film and chill in the fridge for an hour.

Preheat the oven to 200C/400F/Gas 6.

Cut the chilled pastry in half. Roll out one half of the pastry onto a lightly floured work surface to a ?cm/?in thickness. Using a 7cm/2?in pastry cutter, cut out 15-18 discs (as the mixture allows) and place one into each of the muffin tin wells.

Spoon a tablespoon of the mincemeat mixture into each of the mince pie cases and brush the rim of each pastry case with a little beaten egg.

Roll out the remaining pastry onto a lightly floured work surface to a ?cm/?in thickness. Using a 5cm/2in pastry cutter, cut out 15-18 discs and place one on top of each mince pie. Press together the edges of the pastry to seal.

Brush the remaining beaten egg over the tops of the mince pies. Using a knife, make a small steam hole in the top of each pie.

Transfer the mince pies to the oven and bake for 20-25 minutes, or until pale golden-brown.

Serve warm or cold with whipped cream, brandy butter or ice cream.

Hairy Bikers Old Fashioned Minced Pies with an orange crust

Lisa and I have so many things in common, to the point where it is a little bit bonkers. One of the biggies is that we are both completely addicted to cookery books. If you follow us on YouTube, you will have seen us try to narrow down our 5 favourites. Oh my word! It was like picking your favourite child.

One of my favourites and my self-confessed "guilty pleasure" is a book by the Hairy Bikers. I love their style, their passion for food and they make me laugh so much. So in homage to Si & Dave, I have included a recipe from their Christmas Book which I have only just realised is called "The 12 Days of Christmas" – uncanny!

Suggestion: You could double up on the mincemeat recipe and use as gifts. I like to make the mincemeat in advance of making the pies, to allow it to mature.
I have amended some of the quantities.

INGREDIENTS:

- Makes 18 Mince pies
- Ingredients:
- MINCEMEAT
- One lemon, boiled for 1 hour until soft, left to cool
- 100g / 4oz raisins
- 100g / 4oz sultanas
- 1/2 Bramley apple or similar large cooking apple, peeled and chopped

DIRECTIONS:

For the mincemeat, cut the boiled, cooled lemon in half and discard the pips.

Blend the lemon, raisins, sultanas, chopped apple, mixed fruit and mixed peel in a food processor to a paste.

Transfer the lemon mixture to a large mixing bowl and add the suet, muscavado sugar, currants, cinnamon, nutmeg, mixed spice, ground ginger, brandy and sherry. Mix together until well combined, then set aside overnight.

For the orange pastry, grease one large or two small muffin tins with butter. (You will need a tin with 15-18 wells.)

Preserved Lemons

Occasionally when I have one lemon on my shopping list, I will buy a net and use the spares for preserving. They make a fabulous looking (and tasty) gift and a great addition to dishes like a tagine or a couscous. See Lisa's recipe for on page 22.

INGREDIENTS:

- **4 x unwaxed small lemons with thin skins**
- **Juice of 2 additional lemons**
- **100g / 4oz sea salt**
- **1-2 tablespoons olive oil**
- **A selection of bay leaves, peppercorns, a dried chilli, seeds (cumin, coriander or cloves)**
- **1 large or 2 small jars with lids – sterilised.**

DIRECTIONS:

Wash the lemons, then make a deep cut into the lemon from the top as if you are quartering it, but only cut 2/3 of the way down the lemon and then turn the lemon 45 degrees and repeat.

Cut all of the lemons in the same way.
Pack the salt into the lemons, then pack the lemons into the jars, with the cut side up (facing the opening in the jar). Add the seasoning to the jar so that they look attractive.

Make the brine. Boil some water and pour into the jars to cover the lemons, fill to the top. Secure the lid and give a shake to release any air pockets.

During the next 3 -4 week continue to shake the lemon jars.

To use: remove a lemon from the jar and wash off the brine. Remove the flesh and discard. Use the lemon rind sliced or chopped finely in your dishes.

They will keep in the fridge for 6 – 9 months. After the first use, add some of the olive oil to the surface of the water and this will stop any mould forming.

Chocolate Truffles

I would love to be given these truffles as a gift – just saying.
Jane x

INGREDIENTS:

- **175g / 6oz plain dark chocolate (min. 70%cocoa)**
- **100ml / 4 fl oz double cream**
- **4 tablespoons orange liqueur (ie Grand Marnier)**
- **1 unwaxed orange – skin finely grated**
- **175g / 6oz plain chocolate**
- **Cocoa powder**

DIRECTIONS:

Line a baking sheet or tray with non-stick baking parchment.

Break 175g dark chocolates into bits.

In a saucepan, bring the cream to the boil.

Remove from the heat and add the chocolate, orange rind and orange liqueur.

Stir well until all of the ingredients are combined. Cool and then chill for 15 minutes.

Beat the mix with a wooden spoon for about 5 minutes, the texture will be like fudge.

Roll into even sized small balls and place on the baking tray. When all of the mix has been used, freeze for one hour.

Heat some water in a small pan with a bowl over it (but not touching the water). Break the other 175g of dark chocolate and melt in the bowl. Using a couple of teaspoons, dip each truffle into the melted chocolate and coat. If you like cocoa, as the chocolate begins to set is the time to coat the truffle into the cocoa. Repeat with all of the truffles.

Keep refrigerated until you want to use, they will keep for a week.

Tangerine Curd

Homemade curd is the best– I don't think there is any that we would turn away. This variation makes a delicious addition to the Christmas morning breakfast table, but also make such an attractive gift!

Remember, patience is virtue when t comes to making curd.

INGREDIENTS:

- **10 – 12 tangerines (depending upon size) Unwaxed would be great if you can find them**
- **2 lemons**
- **500g /1lb caster sugar**
- **100g / 4oz unsalted butter**
- **5 x fresh medium size free range eggs**

DIRECTIONS:

Wash and sterilise 6 jars and lids ready for the curd.

Wash the tangerines well and then grate the skin using the fine side of a grater. Juice the fruit and pass through a fine nylon sieve.

Juice the lemon. Put the lemon juice, tangerine juice and peel, sugar, butter and sugar into a heat proof bowl.

In a separate bowl crack and then beat the eggs. Stain them into the juice mixture.

Bring a saucepan of water to the boil and then to a simmer. Place the bowl over the hot water, but make sure that the base of the bowl is NOT touching the water.

Now is the time to put the podcast on that you have been meaning to listen to.

Start stirring with a wooden spoon and continue until the mix is thick and coats the back of your wooden spoon.

Please do not rush this bit, if you overheat the curd it will curdle. You won't be sorry as this is a delicious curd.

Pour into the sterilised jars and seal.

Foodies Note:
A teaspoon of this curd with fresh yogurt and granola (page 41) is highly recommended!

Roasted Garlic in Olive Oil

A perfect gift for a food lover, particularly for a garlic lover! Add a tag or card with suggestions on how to use. Try our Red Pepper Dip (page 15)

INGREDIENTS:

- **6 – 8 heads of garlic**
- **Approximately 300ml good quality olive oil**
- **1 x tablespoon of additional oil for roasting**
- **Dried bay leaves**
- **Sprigs of rosemary**
- **Presentation jars that are attractive for gifting.**

DIRECTIONS:

First sterilise your jars and lids.

Preheat your oven to 180'c / 350'f / Gas mark 4

Wash the rosemary sprigs and allow to dry completely.

Remove the papery outer skins from the garlic bulbs and place on a baking tray with a tablespoon of oil.

Roast for 15-20 minutes according to the size of the garlic bulbs. Using a fine skewer, check that the bulb is cooked, lovely and soft, but not mushy. Cook for a further few minutes if needed.

Move to a board and allow to go cold.

Using a really sharp knife or shears, carefully trim off the top 1cm and discard the trimmings.

Tightly pack the garlic bulbs into your sterilised jar/jars along with a bay leaf and a sprig of the washed rosemary. Cover then completely with olive oil. Seal, label and decorate the jar. The garlic will keep in a 'fridge for about 3 months.

Foodie Notes

Suggestions for use: delicious used for garlic bread, pizza bases, bruschetta ..... Love it with roast lamb or lamb steaks, or one in a chicken cavity Barbecued is delicious. The oil that is left is amazing and can be used for so much. I think it is a shame to heat it, I love it in vinaigrettes and dressings.

Boozy Apple Cider, page 44

Roasted Garlic in Olive Oil, page 47

Tangerine Curd page 48

Pumpkin and Cranberry Jam

In the interest of full disclosure, I (Jane)think that I need to admit now that I consider myself part American. I think this recipe would make a wonderful addition to the Thanksgiving table as well as a Christmas gift!

INGREDIENTS:

- *1 kg / 2lb pumpkin (prepared weight)*
- *225g / 9oz cranberries (fresh or frozen)*
- *1 lemon*
- *Water*
- *1.250kilo / 2 ½ lb granulated sugar*

DIRECTIONS:

Prepare the pumpkin. Peel and remove the seeds. Dice.

Sterilise 6 jars and lids ready for your jam.

Put the pumpkin dice and cranberries into a preserving pan. Juice the lemon and add to the pan along with 250ml /1/2 pint of water.

Bring gradually to the boil and simmer covered, until the pumpkin is soft. Stir occasionally to make sure that the mix does not stick to the bottom of the pan.

Add the sugar and stir until completely dissolved. Bring to a hard boil and when very thick pot and seal. Do not overboil as the mix could caramelise.

Delicious served with turkey!

Hot 'n Boozy Apple Cider

You know how much I love a cocktail, so it's probably not a huge surprise that I've put this recipe here! The best part is you've got a mocktail AND a cocktail in one recipe -- just leave out the bourbon if you're serving this to those who prefer mocktails.

INGREDIENTS:

- **4 cups fresh apple cider**
- **1 orange, cut in half**
- **2 cinnamon sticks**
- **2 star anise**
- **4-6 cardamom pods**
- **1 teaspoon freshly grated nutmeg**
- **1 shot of bourbon per glass (Bulleit and Four Roses are my favs)**

DIRECTIONS:

Combine all the ingredients in a heavy Dutch oven and bring to a boil.

Turn down the heat, simmer on low for 20-30 minutes. Be sure to simmer on the lowest setting because you don't want all the goodness evaporating!

If you don't want to fish out all the spices, you can strain before serving. Or put the star anise and cardamom pods in a cheesecloth or tea infuser ball.

Serve hot in mugs.

Stir in one shot of bourbon and enjoy!

Gifts for the Keen Cook

I love the idea of blending spices and herbs and gifting them to the keen cook. I would be delighted to receive this personal gift and you can choose a blend suiting the style of cooking for the chef. Spicy, Asian, Cajan, Mediterranean etc…

Think about containers to hold them, there are some fantastic finds in antique centres, to make the gift even more exciting.

If you go to a wholefood shop or deli' and buy the spices loose buy weight, you will find it a lot more economical. Here are some suggestions:

Mixed Spice
Perfect for the baking enthusiast or a hot chocolate fan!
2 tablespoon whole allspice
2 tablespoon coriander seed
4 tablespoon cloves
4 blades of mace
2 teaspoon ground ginger
4 teaspoon ground nutmeg
Cinnamon stick.

Combine all the spices, break the cinnamon stick into pieces. Grind to a find powder in a pestle and mortar or if you have a one a spice grinder. A coffee grinder also works wonderfully. Pack and seal into individual packets and pop into containers if using.

Garam Masala Blend:
4 tablespoon cardamom pods
1 cinnamon stick
2 tablespoon coriander seeds
4 tablespoons black peppercorns
2 teaspoons cloves
2 tablespoon cumin seeds

Combine all of the spices into a bowl, break the cinnamon stick into pieces.

Grind to a fine powder in a pestle and mortar, spice or coffee grinder.

Seal in individual packets and label.

Homemade Granola

This is great to have on hand for your hungry houseguests, or when you're going to a holiday party and need to bring a gift. It's delicious to snack on, or topped with yogurt and fresh fruit!

If you're giving it as a gift, put it in a festive mason jar, tied with Christmas ribbon. Or put it in a fun basket and tuck in tins of tea and the cocoa mix with gingerbread marshmallows (pg. 35)

INGREDIENTS:

- *1 cup quick cooking oats*
- *1 cup shredded unsweetened coconut*
- *1 cup almonds*
- *1 cup pecans*
- *1 cup pumpkin seeds*
- *1 cup sunflower seeds*
- *1/4 cup flax seeds*
- *1/4 cup chia seeds*
- *1/4 cup hemp seeds*
- *1/4-1/2 cup golden raisins*
- *4 teaspoons ground cinnamon*
- *1 teaspoon freshly grated nutmeg*
- *1 teaspoon ground cardamom*
- *1 teaspoon vanilla extract*
- *2 teaspoons Maldon salt*
- *1/2 cup maple syrup*

DIRECTIONS:

Preheat oven to 300 degrees F.

In a food processor, pulse together the oats, coconut, almonds, pecans, pumpkin seeds, sunflower seeds, flax, chia, hemp and raisins. Pulse a few times to create a loose, granola bar texture.

Add mixture to a large bowl and stir in cinnamon, vanilla extract, spices, salt and maple syrup. Stir well to incorporate all the ingredients together.

Spoon mixture onto a parchment lined rimmed baking sheet. Use a spatula to spread the mixture evenly on the baking sheet.

Bake for about 20-30 minutes, until the granola is a deep golden brown color. I highly recommend rotating the pan halfway through baking.

Let cool, then break into large chunks. Serve with your favorite yogurt and fresh fruit.

When my son George was little, we would meet regularly with a group of Mums and children. We called ourselves "Go Kiss a Peach" – an anagram of the first names from all of the children in the group. At Christmas we would meet in my kitchen to make these biscuits (minus the sherry).

We would make them into tree decorations and gifts and of course, we would eat the rest!

There are a lot of spices in these biscuits, and I recommend finding a deli' or wholefood shop that sells spices by the weight. It will work out a lot cheaper than buying jars. Just remember to write on the packet what the spice is.

St. Nicholas Biscuits

INGREDIENTS:

- *350g / 12 oz plain flour*
- *1 tablespoon baking powder*
- *1 tablespoon ground cinnamon*
- *1 teaspoon ground cloves*
- *1 teaspoon ground nutmeg*
- *½ teaspoon ground aniseed*
- *½ teaspoon ground ginger*
- *250g / 9oz unsalted butter*
- *100g / 4 oz caster sugar*
- *125 g / 4oz dark brown sugar*
- *50ml (2fl oz) sherry*
- *Christmas shaped cookie cutters.*
- *Baking trays and parchment to line.*

DIRECTIONS:

Heat your oven – 180'c / 350'f / gas mark 4
Sift the flour in to a bowl and then mix in the baking powder and spices.

Beat the butter and sugar together until soft and creamy, then beat in the dry ingredients. Add the sherry, then bring everything together into a ball of dough.

Roll out to biscuit thickness on a lightly floured board and cut out your chosen shapes. Place on the parchment on a baking tray. If you are making decorations for a tree, use a skewer to make the hole for the ribbon. Don't worry if this closes up when the biscuit grows in the over. You can re-open the hole after cooking.

Cook in your pre heated oven for about 15 minutes. Remove from the oven and allow to cool on the tray before moving to a cooling rack.

Decorate your biscuits with icing and as many gaudy decorations as you fancy. I love going to town. Tie the ribbon through the hole ready to attach them to the tree.

If a gift, line a pretty tin with tissue and or parchment and add your home made biscuits.

EDIBLE GIFTS

DIRECTIONS CONT'D:

Working quickly, slide the pan off the heat and start whisking the egg whites on a medium/fast speed until stiff peaks form.

Drain the softened gelatine and blot dry on a clean tea towel. Add to the hot syrup and combine quickly with a rubber spatula.

With the mixer on slow/medium speed, pour the hot syrup on to the egg whites in a slow and steady stream. Take care not to pour onto the moving whisk, you do not want splatter. Be careful, this syrup is hot hot hot. The egg whites will foam as the hot syrup is added.

Increase the speed and whisk for a further 3-4 minutes, until the mixture is thick and glossy. Add the spices and whisk for 5 seconds to combine.

Pour the marshmallow into the prepared tin and spread level. Leave to cool to room temperature then cover with clingfilm and then cover for 4 hours or overnight until firm.

Tip the reserved icing sugar mix onto a baking tray. Turn the marshmallow out of the tin and on to the baking tray and carefully peel off the lining paper. Use a greased knife to cut into pieces, tossing each piece into the icing sugar mix as you do so.

The marshmallows will keep for up to one week in an air tight box.

Homemade Gingerbread Marshmallows

INGREDIENTS:

- *Makes 30*
- *Ingredients:*
- *Sunflower oil for greasing*
- *2 tablespoons icing sugar*
- *2 tablespoons cornflour*
- *6 leaves – platinum grade gelatine*
- *2 large egg white*
- *200g / 8oz caster sugar*
- *Pinch of salt*
- *2 teaspoons ground ginger*
- *½ teaspoon ground cinnamon*
- *Generous pinch of ground allspice*
- *Generous pinch of ground cloves*
- *Generous grating of nutmeg*
- *100g / 4oz light soft brown sugar*
- *2 tablespoons molasses or black treacle*
- *2 tablespoons golden syrup*
- *20cm Square baking tin*
- *Sugar thermometer*

A luxurious "hot chocolate" deserves special marshmallows. This is a recipe from "Sweet Things" created by Annie Rigg. They make a special gift, are delicious toasted, but "WOW" with a hot choc!

I recommend reading through the recipe before you start making. It helped me.

DIRECTIONS:

Lightly grease the baking tin with sunflower oil, line with non-stick baking parchment and lightly grease the parchment. In a small bowl, combine the icing sugar and cornflour. Dust the inside of the lined tin with a tablespoon or so of the icing sugar mix.

Place the gelatine leaves in a bowl, cover with cold water and leave to soak and soften while you prepare the rest of the ingredients.

Place the egg whites in the clean bowl of a free-standing mixer fitted with whisk attachment. Add 1 tablespoon of the caster sugar and salt, but do not start whisking yet. Mix all of the spices together in a small bowl.

Tip the remaining caster sugar, soft light brown sugar, molasses, and golden syrup into a medium sized saucepan. Add 150ml water and set over a medium heat to dissolve the sugar. Bring to the boil and cook gently and steadily until the syrup reaches 120'c/248'f on the sugar thermometer.

Rich and Velvety Hot Chocolate with Homemade Gingerbread Marshmallows

Love a hot chocolate, particularly on Christmas Eve. Cream is a must. This recipe is a little bit more decadent and we wholly encourage you to go for it!

INGREDIENTS:

- *Serves 4*
- *Ingredients*
- *800ml (200ml / 7fl oz per person) whole milk (semi-skimmed is fine if that is what you have in the fridge)*
- *200g / 8oz good quality milk chocolate*
- *100g / 4oz dark chocolate (80% cocoa)*
- *½ teaspoon vanilla paste*
- *200g /8oz double cream*
- *See optional extras below*

DIRECTIONS:

Whip the double cream to the point where it will hold its shape. Do not overwhip or it will not be easy to pipe on the surface of your hot chocolate. Put into a piping bag and keep in the refrigerator until later.

Add your milk to a saucepan.

Grate the dark and milk chocolate. Set aside a little to decorate the cream. Add the rest to the milk along with the vanilla.

On a medium heat, stir until the chocolate has melted and the mix has reached a pleasant temperature for drinking. If you want to add optional extras, this is your opportunity. (see foodie notes)

Pour into 4 tall Christmas mugs.

Pipe the cream onto the surface of the hot chocolate, sprinkle with the retained chocolate and serve with marshmallows.

Optional extras:

- Add a healthy pinch of cinnamon
- Add a pinch of chilli
- Add a slug of rum
- Add a slug of Baileys Cream Liqueur
- Add a slug of an orange liqueur
- Lisa adds a slug of eggnog. I personally need to be convinced by this one!

Candy Cane Cookies

My kids LOVED making these every year! One of my favorite holiday traditions with them!

INGREDIENTS:

- *1 cup butter, softened*
- *1 cup confectioners' sugar*
- *1 egg*
- *2 teaspoons peppermint extract*
- *1 teaspoon vanilla extract*
- *1/2 teaspoon salt*
- *2 1/2 cups all-purpose flour, sifted, plus an extra 1/4 cup1/2 teaspoon red food coloring*

DIRECTIONS:

In a stand mixer, cream butter and confectioners' sugar until light and fluffy, 5-7 minutes.

Beat in egg, peppermint extract, vanilla, and salt. With the mixer on low, slowly blend sifted flour into mixture in several small additions. Beat until just combined. If the dough is too sticky and wet, add more flour 1 tablespoon at a time.

Remove half the dough from the bowl, place in a separate bowl and cover with a damp kitchen towel. The kitchen towel will prevent the dough from drying out as you work.

Add red food coloring into the half remaining in the bowl and mix until the coloring is evenly distributed throughout the dough.

Cover the red dough with a damp kitchen towel. Use a floured teaspoon to measure 1 teaspoon each of white and red dough for each cookie.

On a lightly floured surface roll each piece of dough into a 4" rope shape. Place a red and white rope side-by-side, press together lightly and twist to form a spiral. Place on ungreased cookie sheet. Gently curve top down to form handle of a candy cane.

Bake until set, about 9 minutes.
Immediately remove cookies from cookie sheet. Cool on a rack.

Soda Bread

This makes one good sized loaf or make into smaller rolls. If you have bits on bobs left in the fridge, you can add these to the bread mix – chopped up olives, or thinly shredded sundried tomatoes. Or sprinkle the top with oats or seeds.

It's a great stand by recipe to have in your kitchen if you run out of bread during the holiday. Simple to make and goes down a treat with a bowl of soup.

INGREDIENTS:

- **500g plain white flour/all-purpose flour**
- **2 teaspoon bicarbonate of soda/baking soda**
- **1 x teaspoon salt**
- **400ml Natural live yogurt (or buttermilk if you can get some)**
- **A little milk.**
- **Preheat an oven to 200 degrees c./ Gas mark 6**

DIRECTIONS:

Combine all of the dried ingredients in a large bowl and make sure that they are well mixed. Add the yogurt and any extras that you want to add.

Bring the mix together (if too dry just add a little milk). Work quickly, as soon as the bicarb' hits moisture it will start to work. Remember that this is not a conventional bread, it does not need kneading and will not benefit from over working. Shape into a round loaf put on a baking tray, cut a cross on the top and then into the oven. As simple as that.

Cook for 40-45 mins. If you are making rolls less time is needed.

Vegetable Soup with Cheesy Dumplings and Soda bread

The perfect soup to serve to friends and family after a long walk. After all of the rich food consumed at Christmas, this is a healthy, hearty addition to your menu planning. It is also a great way to use up the vegetables left in the fridge.

INGREDIENTS:

- *Serves 4*
- *Ingredients:*
- *25g / 1oz unsalted butter*
- *1 onion – finely sliced*
- *500g / 1lb mixed vegetables. (eg carrots, turnip, swede, celery, cauliflower, parsnip, potato) slice & dice*
- *1litre /2 pints Vegetable stock*
- *25g / 1 oz pearl barley*
- *1 bouquet garni*
- *Salt and freshly ground black pepper*
- *For the cheesy dumplings:*
- *75g /3oz self-raising flour*
- *25g /1oz shredded suet (make sure you use vegetarian, if feeding someone on a vegetarian diet - i cannot tell the difference!)*
- *50g /2oz mature cheddar cheese, grated*
- *2 tablespoons of milk.*

DIRECTIONS:

Melt the butter in a large saucepan and fry the onions gently for about 2 minutes, until transparent.

Add all of the vegetables, stock, pearl barley and bouquet garni. Bring to the boil and simmer for about 30 mins. Season to taste. While the soup is cooking, make the dumplings.

Mix the flour, suet and cheese and bind with just enough milk to make a soft scone like dough. Shape into about 16 dumplings and pop onto the surface of the simmering soup. Cover the pot and allow to cook for a further 20 minutes,

Serve in large warmed bowls, with a hunk on cheese on the side.

Foodies Notes:

A good substitution for suet is vegetable shortening like Crisco.

Truffle Rosemary Popcorn

Adding truffle salt and fresh rosemary takes popcorn
to a whole new delicious level of flavor!

INGREDIENTS:

- **1 tablespoon coconut oil**
- **1/3 cup popcorn kernels**
- **Truffle salt**
- **1 tablespoon finely chopped fresh rosemary**
- **Melted butter**

DIRECTIONS:

Melt the coconut oil over medium heat in a Dutch oven. If you don't have a Dutch oven, use a heavy bottom pot with high sides. It's really important to use a heavy bottom pot because it will disperse the heat more evenly which will help prevent the kernels from burning.

Add 3 corn kernels, cover and wait for them to pop. Keep the heat on medium low -- you don't want the kernels to burn. When they pop, add the rest of the kernels and remove pan from heat.

Wait 30 seconds, then put the pan back on the heat, and partially cover the pot. When you hear the kernels start popping, gently shake the pan.

The kernels will start popping slowing at first, then speed up, then slow down again. When they slow down, remove from heat.

If you don't have enough room to add the toppings to the pot, pour the popcorn into a large bowl.

Stir in melted butter (I usually start with 3-4 tablespoons, but use less if you want less), a generous sprinkle of truffle salt and the fresh rosemary. Stir with a wooden spoon to incorporate all the ingredients.

Serve immediately in one large bowl or individual bowls, and enjoy on your couch while watching your favorite Christmas movie.

Jane and Lisa's
favorite Christmas movies

Love Actually

Miracle on 34th

Polar Express

Elf

The Holiday

Last Christmas

Bridget Jones Diary

Paddington 2

National Lampoon's Christmas Vacation

Noelle

CHRISTMAS MOVIE NIGHT

Hot Buttered Rum

Whether you've just come in from an afternoon snowball fight, a day on the ski slopes, or you're binge watching Christmas movies, this is guaranteed to warm you up on cold Winter nights. To make this a mocktail, leave out the butter and the rum and add the sugar and spices to a pot of your favorite black tea. If using in tea, I'd cut the sugar by 1/4, unless you like your tea really sweet!

INGREDIENTS:

- *1 stick unsalted butter, softened*
- *2 cups light brown sugar*
- *1 teaspoon ground cinnamon*
- *1/2 teaspoon freshly grated nutmeg*
- *Pinch ground cloves*
- *Pinch salt*
- *Bottle dark rum (in a pinch I've also used Captain Morgan's)*
- *Boiling water*

DIRECTIONS:

In a small bowl, cream together the butter, sugar, cinnamon, nutmeg, cloves, and salt. Refrigerate until almost firm.

Spoon about 2 tablespoons of the butter mixture into 12 small mugs. If you're snowed in and your guests can't make it you can keep the mixture refrigerated. I always like to make a big batch of the mixture to keep on hand, so I'm ready for any drop by guests.

Pour about 3 ounces of rum into each mug. Top with boiling water, stir well and serve immediately.

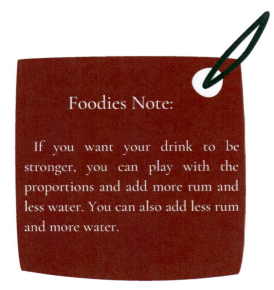

Foodies Note:

If you want your drink to be stronger, you can play with the proportions and add more rum and less water. You can also add less rum and more water.

DIRECTIONS CONT'D:

Oranges: Cut away all the pith from the oranges, carefully segment.

Mix with the chopped fig and scatter over the soaked ginger cake base.

Pour over the chilled custard and refrigerate overnight. You can also begin the syllabub which can refrigerate overnight.

Before serving your trifle, finish the syllabub.

Strain the lemon mixture into a bowl. Add the cream and whip until thick. Put onto the custard mix and swirl around.

Decorate with the macaroons, thin slices of the fig and sprinkle over the crushed amaretto biscuits. Serve and enjoy.

Orange and Fig Trifle

This is luxurious option to the traditional trifle, it is rich but the texture is luscious and light. It is also a tad on the boozy side, so it is guaranteed to impress the in laws!

INGREDIENTS:

- *500ml / 1 pint whole gold top milk*
- *6 large eggs – farm fresh*
- *50g / 2oz caster sugar*
- *2 heaped teaspoons cornflour*
- *1 x vanilla pod*
- *200g / 8oz ginger cake*
- *100ml sherry or amaretto*
- *8 small ripe figs (2 for decoration)*
- *2 oranges*
- *1 lemon*
- *125ml 4 fl oz sweet white wine or substitute with a ginger liqueur*
- *75g / 3oz caster sugar*
- *300ml / 10fl oz double cream*
- *8 x macaroon to decorate the top (one per person) Amaretti biscuits are fine as an alternative*
- *100g / 4oz crushed amaretti biscuits*

DIRECTIONS:

Put the milk into a saucepan. Split the pod and remove the seeds, add both to the milk and heat until steam rises. Set to one side for 30 minutes to infuse.

In a bowl mix the cornflour, sugar and yolks. Slowly start to add the milk stirring constantly. Finish adding and then return the custard mix to the saucepan.

Heat again, stirring continuously until the custard starts to thicken (patience is required) when it coats the back of your stirring spoon, it is ready.

Pour the custard through a sieve into a bowl. Cover the surface with clingfilm or a parchment disk to stop a skin forming and chill.

Slice the ginger cake and add slices to the bottom of the trifle bowl or some in the individual serving dishes if you have chosen this option. Pour over the sherry or amaretto. Finely grate the orange zest and sprinkle onto the sponge. Allow the sponge to soak up the alcohol while the fruit is prepared.

Figs: Lie the fig on it's side and cut a slice out from the widest part (belly) of the fig. Press the slices around evenly around the sides of the serving bowl, so that they look attractive.

Chop the remaining figs.

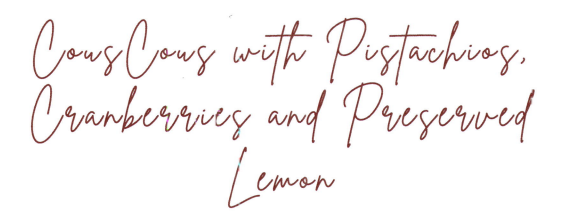

CousCous with Pistachios, Cranberries and Preserved Lemon

This is the perfect make ahead side dish because it truly tastes better after it sits for a bit because that allows all the flavors to really develop.

INGREDIENTS:

- **1 preserved lemon (or 1 regular lemon)**
- **1/2 cup chopped fresh flat-leaf parsley**
- **2 tablespoons butter, room temperature**
- **1/2 cup dried cranberries**
- **1/2 cup unsalted, shelled pistachios, very coarsely chopped (you want nice, bite-sized pieces) (you can also substitute toasted walnuts or toasted slivered almonds)**
- **1 1/4 cups Israeli couscous**
- **salt and pepper to taste**

DIRECTIONS:

Heat the oil in a large, nonstick skillet.

Add the spinach in large handfuls, cooking until it wilts, about 1 minute.

Stir in the garlic, thyme, remaining 1/2 teaspoon salt and ¼ teaspoon pepper. Stir in the Parmesan. Remove from the heat and let cool.

If using a preserved lemon, cut the stem end off and scoop out the inside pulp. Reserve the pulp, and finely dice the rind. If using a regular lemon, grate the rind with a microplane and add to a large bowl. Then add the parsley, butter, dried fruit, pistachios, and salt.

Bring a pot of salted water to boil. Add the couscous and cook for about 8-10 minutes, until it's cooked. When it's done the couscous shouldn't be mushy, and should have a little bite to it. Drain couscous and then add to the large bowl. Stir until all the ingredients are incorporated throughout the couscous. Season with salt and pepper.

Serve at room temperature, or refrigerate if you prefer it chilled.

Honey Dill Sauce

INGREDIENTS:

- **1/4 cup Dijon mustard**
- **3 tablespoons honey**
- **splash of apple cider vinegar**
- **1/3 cup olive oil**
- **3 tablespoons chopped fresh dill OR a generous pinch of the Dill Myrtles Seasonings**

DIRECTIONS:

Combine mustard, honey and vinegar in a small bowl. Slowly whisk in the oil and stir in the chopped dill or dill seasoning.

DIRECTIONS CONT'D:

Then repeat with the second sheet of puff pastry.

You should have 4 rectangles of puff pastry. Place the 4 rectangles on the parchment lined baking sheet.

Remove the salmon fillets from the refrigerator and place on a plate. Brush the tops of the fillets liberally with the butter mustard mixture. Then place each fillet, butter-side down, in the center of a piece of puff pastry.

Spoon half of the cooled spinach over the top of each of the 4 salmon fillets.

Now it's time to wrap the salmon like tasty Christmas presents!

Fold one side of the puff pastry so it covers half the salmon. Brush the top of the puff pastry with egg wash. Fold the next side of the puff pastry so it covers the other half of the salmon and partially covers the top of the puff pastry. You're joining the puff pastry together, so you cover the salmon, and the egg wash will act as the "glue" to seal the flaps of the puff pastry together.

Brush the top with the egg wash. Repeat with the other two side of the the puff pastry, until the salmon is wrapped up like a tasty present.

Just like a present, it doesn't need to be perfect! As long as the salmon is well sealed within the puff pastry with no parts of the salmon showing you will be good to go!!

Use a spatula, or your hands, to gently flip each wrapped filet of salmon over. The seam will be on the bottom.

Brush the tops of the puff pastry with egg wash, then with a sharp knife, score shallow, diagonal lines in each direction in a crosshatch pattern.

Or you could get creative and make an ocean pattern or other fun geometric festive pattern.

Bake the salmon for 20 to 25 minutes, or until the pastry turns golden brown.

Let cool a few minutes on the baking sheet. Serve hot with dill honey mustard.

Salmon En Croute

INGREDIENTS:

- **2 tablespoons unsalted butter**
- **1 tablespoon Dijon mustard**
- **Zest of 2 small lemons about ¾ teaspoon**
- **2 teaspoons kosher salt divided**
- **1 teaspoon black pepper divided**
- **4 teaspoons extra virgin olive oil**
- **8 cups fresh baby spinach**
- **3 cloves garlic minced**
- **zest of 1/2 lemon**
- **4 tablespoons freshly grated Parmesan cheese**
- **2 large egg yolks plus 2 teaspoons water**
-
- **2 sheets frozen puff pastry thawed in the refrigerator**
- **4, 6- ounce/100-150g wild salmon fillets, skin removed**

DIRECTIONS:

Be sure your puff pastry is thawed. If you've forgotten, and it's still in the freezer, no worries! Take it out now before you read any more of the recipe! It will thaw while you prep the rest of the ingredients. How do I know for sure? Because I've forgotten to thaw my puff pastry PLENTY of times!

Place a rack in the center of your oven and preheat the oven to 400 degrees F. /200'C/ Gas mark 6

Line a rimmed baking sheet with parchment paper. This is important because it will make clean up SUPER easy!

In a small bowl, lightly beat the egg yolk with 1 teaspoon water. Set aside.

Melt the butter in a small bowl or saucepan. Stir in the Dijon, lemon zest, 1/2 teaspoon kosher salt, and 1/2 teaspoon black pepper. Set aside.

Heat the oil in a large, nonstick skillet.

Add the spinach in large handfuls, cooking until it wilts, about 1 minute.

Stir in the garlic, thyme, remaining 1/2 teaspoon salt and ¼ teaspoon pepper. Stir in the Parmesan. Remove from the heat and let cool.

Place the first puff pastry on a lightly floured work surface and roll it into a 12×14-inch rectangle /30cm x 36cm

With a sharp knife, cut the puff pastry in half crosswise so you are left with two rectangles that are 12 x 7 inches/30cm x 18cm each.

IMPRESS YOUR IN-LAWS

Brie, Cranberry and Buckwheat Blinis

Canapes are our thing! We love them. They should be dainty but pack a punch of flavour. They always get a reaction. Good grief can they be a nightmare to prepare, particularly if you pick ones that are high maintenance at the last minute!

Try to select a canape that you can prepare as much as possible in advance. To make life even simpler for this recipe, you could ditch the blini and buy in a small cracker.

INGREDIENTS:

- **BLINIS (makes 20)**
- **100g / 4oz buckwheat flour**
- **¼ teaspoon baking powder**
- **¼ teaspoon salt**
- **1 egg**
- **100ml / 4 floz milk**
- **TOPPING:**
- **4 slices of pancetta**
- **Ripe Brie**
- **Cranberry sauce**

DIRECTIONS:

To make the Blinis: Sift the dry ingredients into a bowl. Make a well in the centre.

Separate the egg. Set the egg white to one side in a clean bowl.

Beat the yolk into the milk. Pour this mix into the well of your flour and gradually mix in the flour to the egg/milk. Mix until smooth.

Whisk the egg white to soft peaks and gently fold into your batter.

Heat a griddle or saucepan and onto its surface, brush/spray on a scant layer of oil.

In small batches add a teaspoon of your blinis mix. (*we usually do one test one first*).

Cook until bubbles start to appear and the underside is golden brown.

Turn and cook until the second side is golden. Remove to a cooling rack and start your next batch. Cool.

In advance cook the pancetta in a dry frying pan until crispy. Cook and crumble up to make a topping.

Cut the brie into triangles to fit on the blini.

Up to half an hour before serving, construct your canape. Spread a small amount of cranberry sauce on each blini. Top with the brie. Sprinkle on some Pancetta crumble and serve.

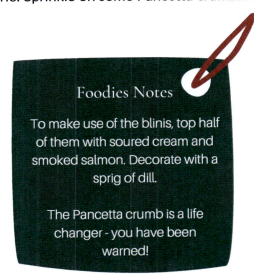

Foodies Notes

To make use of the blinis, top half of them with soured cream and smoked salmon. Decorate with a sprig of dill.

The Pancetta crumb is a life changer - you have been warned!

Roasted Red Pepper
and
Garlic Dip

This is one of the easiest of dips to prepare and it is so delicious. You might want to make extra, it gets gobbled up pretty quickly!

INGREDIENTS:

- *1 x 460-480g jar roasted red peppers*
- *200g /8oz natural full fat Greek yogurt*
- *200g/8oz pack cream cheese*
- *2 cloves roasted garlic - peeled*
- *Sea salt and freshly ground black pepper*
- *Squeeze of lemon juice*
- *Crackers for serving.*

DIRECTIONS:

This uses two cloves from the bulb, recipe on page 47 for "Roasted Garlic". If you haven't roasted garlic, when you next have your oven on at about 180'c, pop a bulb of garlic wrapped in foil on a shelf in your oven to roast for 15 – 20 minutes. Allow to cool and store.

Drain the peppers into a sieve and discard the liquid. Make sure they are well drained. Adding any excess liquid will make your dip runny.

Pop into a food processor along with the cream cheese, yogurt, peeled garlic, and seasoning. Blitz to a dip consistency.

Taste and add some lemon juice and additional seasoning if required.

Serve in a bowl with the crackers placed around.

Note from Jane: Hands up - I am no fan of mayonnaise, but you can subsidise the yogurt for mayo'.

Foodies Notes:
You could use the toasted baguette that we feature on chilli, pecan Camembert recipe on page 117.

If you are gifting the roasted garlic, why not handwrite this recipe in a Christmas card to go with it?

Holiday entertaining is so much fun, and the great thing is you don't need to spend hours in the kitchen to create a fabulous spread for your friends!

A simple charcuterie board, some dips and spreads and, of course cocktails (and mocktails) are festive, fun and incredibly easy to whip up!

Keep an assortment of crackers, cheese, jarred olives and nuts on hand for those spur of the moment "let's have friends over" nights.

If you love having friends over, but dread all the work of planning a dinner, invite your friends over for apps and drinks, instead!

Put on some festive music, light candles and throw a log, or two on the fire. Break out your fancy china and crystal.......you may have to dig to the back of your cupboard, but now is the perfect time to use it!

Cranberry Cheese

The wonderful thing about making preserves like a fruit cheese for Christmas is that it is "one for a gift and one for me!" This fruit cheese is deliciously tart, and compliments rich meat & pâté as well as looking completely at home on a cheese board. A slice of cranberry cheese with some "Stinking Bishop" cheese. Yes please!

INGREDIENTS:

- *1 kilo / 2lb fresh or frozen cranberries*
- *500ml /1 pint water*
- *500g / 1lb granulated sugar*
- *1 x star anise*
- *Sterilise your chosen containers or moulds.*

DIRECTIONS:

Put your fresh or frozen cranberries into a preserving pan with the water & star anise. Bring slowly to a simmer and let the cranberries "pop" and soften. They need to be cooked through.

Remove the star anise, Pass the fruit pulp through a fine nylon sieve and then return to the pan and heat again slowly.

Add the sugar and stir well until the sugar is dissolved. Continue stirring until the cheese is thick and leaving the sides of the pan.

Pot, seal and label.

Foodies note:

If you are serving with a pate – we suggest adding some texture. Pot the cheese into a mould, put a layer of chopped walnuts into the mould first and then the fruit cheese on top. Looks and tastes good.

Chestnut Chutney

This chutney is delicious spread on a small cracker with a tasty cheese. Also fabulous, with bubble and squeak on Boxing Day! Buying pre peeled chestnuts is highly recommended, peeling your own is quite an achievement and we award you a Christmas gold star if you give it a go!

INGREDIENTS:

- *750g / 1.6lb Bramley apples – cored, peeled and chopped into cubes*
- *45og /1lb onions finely chopped*
- *Zest and juice of 3 clementine oranges*
- *100g / 4oz cranberries*
- *100g / 4oz sultanas*
- *800ml /1 1/4pt white wine vinegar*
- *(Substitute for Cider vinegar if you are making this gift for someone with a gluten intolerance).*
- *250g / 9oz Pre cooked chestnuts finely chopped*
- *1 cinnamon stick*
- *6 cloves*
- *2 allspice berries*

DIRECTIONS:

Put your chosen vinegar into a large, heavy based pan.

Put all of your spices into a muslin bag, tie and add to the vinegar. Put all of the ingredients except for the sugar and chestnuts into the pan.

Bring gently to the boil and simmer for about 1 ¼ hours until the mix is soft. Stir in the chestnuts and the sugar and continue to simmer until glossy and gooey.

Sterilise some jars and lids and put the chutney into the jars while still hot and apply lids. Cool and then label.

This chutney will keep for up to 18 months. If you can make it in advance it will be even nicer for Christmas day.

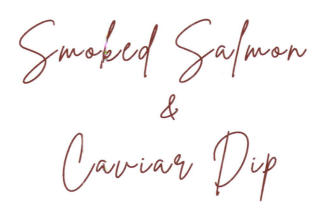

Smoked Salmon & Caviar Dip

This is one of those apps that once you make it, your friends will ask for it again and again. You've been warned! It's also fabulous because you can make it early in the day, or even the day before!

INGREDIENTS:

- **8 ounces/220g cream cheese**
- **4 ounces/110g fresh goat cheese**
- **4 teaspoons finely grated lemon zest**
- **1 pound/460g smoked salmon, skin removed, flaked, divided (use hot smoked or cold smoked)**
- **2 large radishes, trimmed, finely chopped**
- **⅓ cup finely chopped red onion**
- **½ cup drained capers, chopped (if you use the small capers, no need to chop)**
- **3 tablespoons finely chopped chives**
- **Pumpernickel bread, crackers, endive (for serving)**
- **Crème fraîche**
- **Caviar, to garnish**

DIRECTIONS:

Line a 6"-diameter ring mold, 6"-diameter cake pan or spring form pan, or 16-oz. ramekin with plastic wrap, pressing it along the bottom and up the sides, leaving some plastic wrap overhanging the sides. Pulse cream cheese, goat cheese, and lemon zest in a food processor until well combined and very smooth and creamy.

Press a third of smoked salmon into an even layer across the bottom of mold. Spread half of cream cheese mixture evenly over salmon, smoothing surface with a rubber spatula.

Toss radishes and onion in a small bowl to combine, then scatter over cream cheese mixture and, using spatula, press down lightly into mixture. Top with half of remaining salmon, making an even layer, then scatter capers over. Spread remaining cream cheese mixture over capers and finish with a final layer of the remaining salmon.

Using the overhanging plastic wrap, cover dip with plastic wrap and chill at least 1 hour to let dip set and flavors meld.

Uncover dip and carefully invert onto a plate. Remove ring mold, then carefully peel away plastic. Top with a dollop of crème fraîche, caviar and chives.

Serve with endive, pumpernickel bread or crackers.

Shirley Temple

Created by a bar tender in the 1930's it has certainly held the test of time! A fun and easy mocktail.

INGREDIENTS:

- **200ml / 7 fl oz Lemonade, chilled**
- **1 x tablespoon grenadine**
- **Ice**
- **A Maraschino cherry**
- **A slice of orange**
- **Cocktail umbrella – optional**

DIRECTIONS:

Mix the lemonade and grenadine, with the ice in a cocktail shaker.

Pour into a tall glass and garnish with the orange and cherry.

Champagne Pomegranate Cocktail

The Holidays are the PERFECT time to crack open a bottle of champagne! The addition of Aperol makes this a fancier holiday version of an Aperol Spritz. If you prefer Campari, you can absolutely use Campari instead!

INGREDIENTS:

- **1 750 ml bottle of champagne, chilled**
- **1 cup Pomegranate juice, chilled**
- **1 cup Aperol**
- **1/4 cup Pomegranate seeds**
- **4 sprigs of fresh rosemary**

DIRECTIONS:

Put a few pomegranate seeds in the bottom of 6 champagne flutes. Fill each champagne glass 1/2 way with champagne, add a splash of pomegranate and splash of Aperol.

If you want more juice, less champagne, start with the pomegranate juice, then add splash of Aperol and a splash of Champagne.

Garnish with a sprig of fresh rosemary.

FOR A MOCKTAIL VERSION:

Fill a champagne glass 3/4 of the way with club soda, then add a splash of pomegranate juice.

APPETIZERS & COCKTAILS

CONVERSION CHARTS

OVEN TEMPERATURES

gas mark	°C	°F
1	140	275
2	150	300
3	160	325
4	180	350
5	190	375
6	200	400
7	210	425
8	220	450
9	240	475

WEIGHTS

ounces	grams
1	25
2	50
3	75
4	110
5	150
6	175
7	200
8	225
9	250
10	275
11	315
12	350
13	365
14	400
15	425
16/1lb	450

VOLUMES

fluid ounces	millilitres	cups
1/2	15	1 TBL
1	30	1/8
2	60	1/4
2 1/2	75	1/3
4	120	1/2
5	150	2/3
6	180	3/4
8	250	1
9	266	1.10
10	295	1 1/4
15	443	1 3/4
20/1 pint	725	2 1/2
1¼ pints	850	3
1½ pints	1 litre	3 1/2
1¾ pints		4

MENUS

NEW YEAR'S DAY

Mulligawtawny Soup

INGREDIENTS:

- **(serves 6 – but not in my home, because we love this soup so much!)**
-
- **Ingredients:**
- **50g / 2oz unsalted butter**
- **2 leeks, carrots & sticks of celery washed and sliced.**
- **3 cloves garlic – peeled and finely chopped**
- **1 teaspoon ground cumin**
- **½ teaspoon turmeric**
- **1 teaspoon ground coriander**
- **¼ teaspoon chilli flakes**
- **250g /10 oz red lentils**
- **1.3 litre vegetable or chicken stock**
- **Pinch of sea salt**
- **300ml tin coconut milk**
- **A squeeze of lemon or lime juice**
- **Toasted almonds and chopped fresh coriander to serve.**

DIRECTIONS:

Melt the butter in a large saucepan, add the leeks, carrots and celery and sweat for about then minutes until softening, stir occasionally.

Add the garlic and the spices and stir to coat the vegetables. Stir in the lentils.

Pour in the stock, bring to the boil and simmer for about 30 minutes. Stir every now and again, to make sure that it does not catch the bottom of the pan.

Remove from the heat and allow to cool a little before pureeing in a food processor. Do not over fill the blender – trust me, been there, done it and got a soup splatter tea shirt to show for it!

Return the soup to the pan and add the coconut milk. Gently heat, do not boil. Season if needed and add a squeeze of juice.

Serve with scattered toasted almonds and chopped fresh coriander sprinkled over the surface.

Tasty Ham and Cheese Parcel

INGREDIENTS:

- *Serves 4*
- *350g /14oz of quality cooked ham, sliced*
- *100g / 4oz Gruyere cheese – grated*
- *75g / 3oz tasty Cheddar cheese - grated*
- *1 tablespoon Dijon mustard*
- *3 tablespoon crème fraiche*
- *350g / 14oz ready-made butter puff pastry*
- *1 egg*

DIRECTIONS:

Roll out 1/3 of the puff pastry to a rectangle about 30x25cm.

Combine the crème fraiche with the mustard. Spread 1/3 of the mixture over the pastry rectangle, leaving a gap of 1cm on the edges.

Add a layer of ham, half of the mustard mix, all of the cheese and then layer the last of the ham. Finally spread on the last of the mustard mix.

Roll out the remaining pastry, to a larger sized rectangle.

Beat the egg and brush the 1 cm border of the base with egg. Place the pastry lid over and press down the edges to seal. Trim to make neat and then knock up the edges or crimp. Place on a baking tray. Glaze the parcel with the egg. Add a hole in the centre for steam to escape.

Chill until ready to cook.

Preheat the oven to 220'c / 425'f Gas Mark 7

Cook for 25 minutes. Keep an eye on the parcel, if it starts to catch, cover with some foil to protect.

Remove from the oven.

Slice and serve warm so that the cheese is lovely and gooey.

Slow Cooked Shoulder of Lamb

Give me any recipe that involves the words "slow cooked" and I will take it and run with it! For a dinner party or entertaining friends, a slow cooked dish is perfect. All of the preparation, cooking and a lot of the washing up has been done well in advance, giving you the opportunity to enjoy company eating great food.

INGREDIENTS:

- *Serves 6-8*
- *2.5k – 3k should of lamb*
- *500ml / 1 pint chicken stock*
- *100ml / dry white wine*
- *3 fennel bulbs*
- *2 white onions*
- *1 tablespoon of fresh thyme*
- *2 teaspoon fennel seeds*
- *Grated rind of one unwaxed lemon*
- *200ml Madeira Wine*
- *Sea salt and freshly ground black pepper*

DIRECTIONS:

Preheat oven to 160'c / 310'f / gas mark 3

Prepare vegetables: slice the fennel bulbs into wedges that will hold their shape during cooking. Peel and cut the onions into wedges.

DIRECTIONS CONT'D:

Season the joint of lamb and put it in your chosen cooking vessel. Add the stock and white wine. surround the meat with the vegetables Cover with foil or lid. Cook in the oven for 2 hours.

Add the lemon rind, thyme and fennel seeds. Add a bit more stock if needed. Return to the oven covered for another 1 1/2 hours. Check that the meat is succulent and tender. I like to remove the foil 1/2 an hour before cooking to bring a bit of colour to the meat and vegetables.

Remove the lamb to a platter, carefully remove the vegetables and place around the joint and cover with the foil to keep warm.

Strain the juices from the pan, removing the fat from the surface. Add the meat juices to a small saucepan, add the Madeira and simmer to reduce to a wonderfully rich gravy.

Add any juices that have escaped from the lamb to the gravy. Serve alongside the shoulder of lamb and vegetables or drizzle over the lamb in the serving dish. Either way is delicious!

If you have made roasted the garlic (page 47) adding a clove to the gravy is highly recommended!

Should there be any left over (unlikely) shred. Chop the left over veg and add to chicken with some pearl barley to make a fabulous soup

Chili Beef with Salsa and All the Trimmings

Keeping the quality of your New Year's Day in mind, a chilli is a win win. It is a dish that can be made in advance when time is your friend and popped into the freezer. We have included a salsa recipe for you, but why not consider, shop bought tacos, grated cheese, soured cream, all things that can be sourced easily and require very little work.

Think about multiplying the recipe and batch making.

INGREDIENTS:

- *500g / 1lb lean cubed steak*
- *400g tin chopped tomatoes*
- *450ml beef stock*
- *400g tin pinto beans*
- *1 level tablespoon ground cumin*
- *1 x level tablespoon tomato puree*
- *2 x tablespoons vegetable oil*
- *200g / 8 oz red onion chopped*
- *1 large red chilli*
- *1 clove garlic finely chopped*
- *Salt and pepper*
- *Extra chilli powder heat up your chilli if required.*
- *1 tablespoon chopped coriander*

DIRECTIONS:

Heat 1 tablespoon of oil in frying pan. Sweat the onions until soft , the add the garlic, chilli and cumin and cook for a minute. Set them aside in a separate bowl.

Add the remaining tablespoon of oil and start to cook of the beef. Do not overfill the pan or it will not brown. Once you have browned the meat in small batches, add the tomatoes and tomato paste, onion mix and the stock. Bring to the boil then reduce the temperature right down to barely a simmer.

If you have a slow cooker, you could transfer the chilli now to cook on slow for the day. You are wanting the beef to break down and become soft and delicious. It is possible to do this on the hob on the lowest temperature. Stir it occasionally or if you are being mega organised and preparing and slow cooking other dishes, make efficient use of your oven and cook it with these other dishes. Very efficient.

Chill and freeze and pull it out of the freezer the day before it is needed, giving it time to defrost. If you are serving an audience that likes spicy food, add some more chilli.

When needed, add seasoning and bring the chilli back to the boil and simmer on a low heat for 20-30mins.

Sprinkle on the chopped corriander.

Festive Moscow Mule

I think gin also works really well in this. And if want to make it a mocktail leave out the vodka (or gin) and enjoy! If you like an extra minty taste, muddle the mint in your shaker before adding the rest of the ingredients.

INGREDIENTS:

- **Makes 2**
- **4 ounces vodka**
- **juice from 1 lime**
- **1/2 cup pomegranate juice**
- **Fever Tree ginger beer, for topping**
- **pomegranate arils, for serving**
- **fresh mint leaves, for serving**

DIRECTIONS:

Traditionally mules are usually served in copper mugs, but if you don't have a copper mug fill a cocktail glass with ice. It's the holidays, so pull out your fanciest cocktail glasses!

Add vodka, lime juice, pomegranate juice and lots of ice to a cocktail shaker. Shake vigorously for 30 seconds, until the outside of the shaker is too cold to hold and covered in condensation.

Divide between two glasses, and top each glass off with ginger beer.

Garnish with pomegranate arils, a couple sprigs of fresh mint and enjoy.

Blood Orange Cardamom Cake

Winter is blood orange season and I love using them in vinaigrettes, cocktails, marinades and this dessert that tastes like a bite of Winter. It's warm and cozy thanks to the spices, but also has a touch of sweetness with the glaze. It's a great snacking cake or dessert!

INGREDIENTS:

- **Cake:**
- **1/2 cup unsalted Kerrygold (or European) butter, softened**
- **1/2 cup granulated sugar**
- **1/2 cup dark brown sugar**
- **zest of one blood orange (about 1 1/2 tbsp)**
- **2 tbsp blood orange juice**
- **2 eggs**
- **1 tsp vanilla**
- **1 cup sour cream**
- **1 1/2 cups all purpose flour**
- **2 tsp baking powder**
- **1/2 tsp baking soda**
- **1/2 – 1 tsp cardamom (depending on how spicy you want the cake, I usually use 3/4 tsp)**
- **1/4 tsp Saigon cinnamon**
- **1/4 tsp salt**
- **Blood Orange Glaze:**
- **Juice of 1 blood orange (minus the 2 tbsp you use for the cake)**
- **a few drops vanilla extract**
- **1 1/2 – 2 cups powdered sugar**

DIRECTIONS:

Pre-heat oven to 350 degrees.

While your oven is preheating, grease a 10 inch cake pan.

In a large mixing bowl, cream together butter, sugars and orange zest until pale and fluffy. Add in eggs, one at a time. After you add the first egg, beat well before you add the second egg. Use a spatula and scrape down the sides of your bowl. Give the mixture one more blend, and then add vanilla extract and orange juice.

Beat until really light and fluffy; about 2-3 minutes.

In a medium bowl, whisk together flour, salt, baking soda, baking powder, cinnamon and cardamom to combine.

Add 1/3 of the flour mixture to the wet ingredients and mix on low until the it's just barely combined. Add in 1/2 of the sour cream and mix until just combined. You want to make sure you don't over mix at this point. By just barely combining the dry ingredients and sour cream, you'll ensure your cake is nice and fluffy. Repeat this process with the remaining flour and sour cream ending with the last 1/3 of flour mixture.

Use a spatula and scrape down the sides of the bowl (hou don't want to leave any of that goodness on the sides of your bowl!) and beat on low speed until there are no lumps in your batter, but don't over-mix.

DIRECTIONS CONT'D:

Pour batter into prepared cake pan and place on the center rack of your oven to bake for 35-45 minutes or until the center of the cake is set to the touch or a skewer comes out clean when inserted in the center.

Remove from oven and allow the cake to cool for at least 20 minutes in the pan. Then turn the cake out onto a wire rack and allow it to cool completely to room temperature.

While the cake is cooling, prepare your glaze.

Whisk together orange juice, vanilla and powdered sugar until smooth and there aren't any lumps. You want it to be a thick, yet pourable consistency, similar to a pancake batter.

Once your cake is cooled completely pour glaze on the top of the cake and allow glaze to drip over the edges.